LAND OF THE
PILGRIMS' PRIDE

THE WORKS OF GEORGE JEAN NATHAN

THE AUTOBIOGRAPHY OF AN ATTITUDE*
THE AMERICAN CREDO (*Vols.* I *and* II *in collaboration with* H. L. *Mencken*)
THE NEW AMERICAN CREDO*
THE WORLD IN FALSEFACE*
THE HOUSE OF SATAN*
LAND OF THE PILGRIMS' PRIDE
EUROPE AFTER 8:15* (*in collaboration with Mencken*)
THE POPULAR THEATRE
MR GEORGE JEAN NATHAN PRESENTS
COMEDIANS ALL**
ANOTHER BOOK ON THE THEATRE
THE THEATRE, THE DRAMA, THE GIRLS
MATERIA CRITICA
THE CRITIC AND THE DRAMA*
A BOOK WITHOUT A TITLE
BOTTOMS UP
HELIOGABALUS*** (*in collaboration with Mencken*)

In Collaborative Compilations

ESSAYS BY PRESENT-DAY WRITERS, *edited by Raymond Woodbury Pence*
READINGS FROM "THE AMERICAN MERCURY," *edited by Grant C. Knight*
A PORTFOLIO OF AMERICAN EDITORS, *edited by Louis Evan Shipman*
CIVILIZATION IN THE UNITED STATES, *edited by Harold Stearns*

Prefaces

THE MOON OF THE CARIBBEES AND OTHER PLAYS, *by Eugene O'Neill*
HOW'S YOUR SECOND ACT?, *by Arthur Hopkins*
CHICAGO, *by Maurine Watkins*

BOOKS ON MR. NATHAN

THE THEATRE OF GEORGE JEAN NATHAN, *by Isaac Goldberg, Ph.D.*
PISTOLS FOR TWO, *by Owen Hatteras*

* Also published in Great Britain
** Also published in Australia
*** Also published in Germany

LAND OF THE PILGRIMS' PRIDE

GEORGE JEAN NATHAN

Mcmxxvii

New York   ALFRED·A·KNOPF   London

CONTENTS

LAND OF THE
PILGRIMS' PRIDE

THE NEW MORALITY

§ 1

The Change in Morals.—The historian who will set himself to chronicle the salient change in sex morals that has come over the United States in these years of the Twentieth Century will be impressed by one or two phenomena which have been omitted from various recent disquisitions on the subject. One of these is the manner in which that change has affected the American social classes of the second and even third level. That a looseness of sex morals is always more or less a characteristic of the rich and leisurely class in any country is, of course, sufficiently known. In any period this stratum of society is found to suffer less from moral inhibitions than any other, and for obvious reasons. In the first place, it is, by virtue of its position and affluence, able to afford an indifference to the moral and ethical standards prevailing among the less fortunate classes. In the second place, its manner of life is conducive to lax moral standards. And in the third place, its opportunities for pleasure, whether of a sexual nature or otherwise, are manifestly greater than those of the classes which are poorer in the world's goods and hence in leisure. So much is platitude. And platitude, too, is the fact that the classes below this class must inevitably and arbitrarily obey a more rigorous moral code whether they wish to or not, since they must conduct themselves in such wise that the upper class, upon which they depend for a livelihood, may, as the word goes, respect them. Whatever the character of the boss, he expects his clerks to be abstemious, prudent, honorable and moral. This is not so much hypocrisy on the employer's part as it is sound business sense, and not only sound business policy but, on a wider basis, sound social policy. The king may have a dozen mistresses, but his chamberlain must be a respectable married man with one wife, ten children and a pew in the kirk.

The upper class in America, employing the phrase in its broadest sense and including therein those of a relative financial, social and professional eminence, is perhaps more restrained in sex matters than the upper classes of most European nations, excepting only the German, but, even so, the earthquake in sex morals that has shaken the world since the war has affected it to a remarkable degree. Never before in the history of the country's biological conduct has this class of Americans shown a decline in the old moral order as it shows it today. The puritanical attitude toward sex which it periodically displayed up to within a dozen years ago is rapidly disappearing. Today, its philosophical attitude inclines more and more toward the Latin. When I refer to this class, I speak of it, of course, as a whole. There are frequent instances of rebellion against its changed attitude on the part of certain of its component parts and the public prints are often a battleground upon which these upholders of the old tradition plant their thundering Busy Berthas, but, taking it generally, it no longer parades in the moral theatrical whiskers of Josh Whitcomb and the moral eyeglass of Archibald Carlyle. The moralists of the country are not recruited from this

3

class, save on rare occasions; they come from the lower classes. Where one John D. Rockefeller, Jr., or one Henry Ford still shows his mind to be dressed in Sunday-go-to-meeting clothes, there are a thousand men who no longer for a minute think of discharging the cook for a peccadillo with the gendarmerie, of worrying over the unchristian sex morality of the Zulus or of hiding *La Vie Parisienne* under the pillow. Even though he be himself circumspect in his anatomical conduct, the American of the class in point no longer works up the indignation that his father worked up when a neighbor is caught in a moral *faux pas*. He may, true enough, cease to have business dealings with the fellow for a while, since the American business office is still twice as timid, fearful and compulsorily puritanical as the American boudoir, but he has no personal animus against him as he once had. Ostracism for sexual dereliction today operates very feebly in the Republic in so far as its upper class is concerned. There may be a bit of social nervousness in certain instances, but it passes very quickly. The late Cathcart unpleasantness was brought about not by the nobility and gentry, but

4

by self-seeking shysters and their constituents. And, since almost all the important newspapers in America are owned by Americans of the upper class, one found that, without a single exception, they gallantly offered their editorial arms to the lady in distress. I ask but a single question, and that a short one. Would these same newspapers have exhibited the same attitude in a similar or relatively similar situation twenty years ago? The answer is obvious.

All this is merely preamble to the point I am getting at. In America, as in every country under the sun, the so-called inferior classes imitate the upper classes in so far as they can. They imitate these upper classes in dress, in deportment, in pleasures, in thought and in every other way that they are, within the possibilities of their means, able to. In most countries, this cuckooing cannot go very far, since the lesser classes lack the necessary money and leisure. In America, however, the so-called middle class has, in the last fifteen years, acquired money and a consequent share of leisure in an unheard of and amazing degree. Today, it is the richest middle class in the world. And, as a result, it has been able to imitate the upper class of the country more closely than such an imitation has ever before been possible. Thus we find this middle class of Americans presently exhibiting an attitude toward sex morals largely of a piece with that exhibited by its superiors. The middle class I allude to is, plainly enough, that of the larger cities. If the middle classes of the rest of the country have not yet taken color from the former's changed attitude, they may be expected to do so in due time, as the hinterland, however independent of the cities it may be politically and alcoholically, is ever a vassal to the cities' dictate and prejudice in the matter of everything from radio music and moving pictures to store clothes and the philosophy of prophylactic sprays.

A second fact that will impress itself upon the historian of modern sex is the perhaps deplorable practicability of a moderate lack of chastity on the part of the present-day young woman. To put the matter delicately, the virgin today stands infinitely less chance of grabbing off a meritorious husband than her slightly lax sister. She gets a husband, true enough, but what kind? Generally some very

young idiot or some more adult sentimental ass. The
day of the romance of the chaste young woman appears slowly to be vanishing; men no longer view
her as the desirable goddess of the past. Chastity
alone is no longer the excellent bait that it once was.
Other qualities are demanded in a woman, and are
regarded as vastly more important, and are more
efficient in roping and pulling in the marrying
male. I do not mean to justify a young woman's
looseness in sex morals; that is certainly far from
my purpose; all that I wish to do is to point out,
and perhaps even lament, the undeniable fact that
the not too circumspect girl of today pretty generally gets a much better grade of husband for herself than the girl who obeys the injunction of
Marie Lloyd's familiar music hall ditty. Why this
should be, I don't know. I can only guess at a few
of the reasons. The first of these, as I have already
suggested, is that the virtuous woman usually attracts the mentally inferior man. There are exceptions, but as a general thing men of experience
and wisdom and humor are more greatly drawn
to the woman who, too, has had a share, however
small, of the world's experience, wisdom and

7

humor. In such a woman they find the ready sympathy, quick perception and companionship that they fail to find in the average immaculate maiden. Sex may be a second, third or even tenth consideration; it may hardly enter the man's consciousness; he may, indeed, have no relations with the woman; but instinctively he sees in her and feels in her an understanding and a comradeship that he fails to find in the vestal. The foundation of modern civilization rests on the contrary assumption. But the bricks are loosening in an alarming manner.

Reverting momentarily to one phase of the subject matter of the introductory paragraphs, to wit, the change in the American attitude toward sex as it operates today on its higher levels, I may confidently anticipate ironic objection from readers in what will be announced to be incontrovertible proof to the contrary through the citation of various recent and conspicuous court decisions in cases of sexual misdemeanor. As an illuminating illustration, these readers will doubtless quote, among other instances, the late action of the Appellate division of the Supreme Court of New York in the instance of a divorce case which, upon its original trial, resulted in the presiding justice indignantly taking the case from the jury and ordering a verdict in favor of the accused wife. In this case, the higher court reversed the earlier judgment and directed a new trial, clearly implying that—and this is the point my readers will unquestionably emphasize—the attitude of the community toward women's conduct on the borderland of sex had not changed as the attorneys for the accused wife and subsequently the lower court had maintained. That there is any real significance in this or in any other court decision or observation like it and that it is in any way accurately reflective of the prevailing attitude toward and philosophy of sex, I allow myself seriously to doubt. If there is any way to judge what that attitude and philosophy are, it lies in a contemplation not of judges, but of juries. And a scrutiny of the actions of juries in cases where women are accused of sexual dereliction today vouchsafes a quite different story. It is getting to be as difficult to find a jury of twelve middle class Americans that will condemn a woman for a violation of the moral code as it is to find one that will convict a man for a violation of the Eighteenth

Amendment. The situation was different twenty years ago, even fifteen years ago. But if, today, my readers can prove to me that, in any part of America, there is more than one jury out of every fifty that has or will cast its vote against a woman charged with a violation of the Seventh Commandment, I shall be happy to retract the whole of my contention and to supplement the retraction with a box of first-class cigars.

Nor is the present attitude of juries based, I believe, upon sentimental reasons. Now and again, of course, twelve good jackasses and true may surrender their common sense to a head of pretty blonde hair, a pug nose, a baby stare and a chiffon collar, but very, very few of the fair accused are found to have heads of pretty blonde hair, pug noses, baby stares and chiffon collars. The average woman who sits in the witness-box accused by her husband of having allowed a bond broker or a movie actor to have his way is, if the art of photography isn't a liar, generally observed to be in face and figure sister to the prune strudel. There is approximately as much sex appeal to her, in the case of the prosaic gentlemen of the jury,

10

as there is to their mothers-in-law. Yet their findings are the same in the case of such a creature;
they decline to lift a blue-nose against her. It is not
sentiment, as I have said, nor is it chivalry, for the
average American is certainly less sentimental and
less chivalrous today than his father was. I doubt
that anyone will go so far as to deny that. It is
simply that he has come to look upon sexual lapses
no longer as a heinous thing; it is simply that at
least that much of the philosophy of Jesus Christ
has at last penetrated into the consciousness of
Homo Americanus.

§ 2

The Question of Virtue.—Nothing is more clearly
indicative of this change in sex morals which has
come over the Anglo-American world than man's
present attitude toward woman's virtue, already
briefly alluded to. Up to comparatively recent
years, the question of a woman's virtue was an even
greater consideration on the part of the man contemplating marriage with her than her culinary
skill, the cleanliness of her hair and her father's
police record. The woman who had succumbed to

11

some knave's wiles was not only sidestepped by the matrimonially inclined male, but was looked upon by other women as a creature headed for the eternal fires. She was, in a word, morally and socially *déclassée*. The novels and plays of the era invariably dealt with her in much the same manner, to wit, as one either to be scorned or pitied. Such was the situation up to within no more than ten or fifteen years ago. Then, suddenly, there came an abrupt change. Not only was comparative lack of virtue no longer held against a woman; it was actually looked on with favor and endorsed. So much so, indeed, that today things have come to such a point that the so-called virgin is actually a subject for esoteric mirth and jeer not only on the part of men but also on the part of women, and not only on the part of women, but, what is more, on the part of the unhappy creature herself. She is not proud of her virtue, as she once was, but actually ashamed of it.

The virtuous woman no longer holds the pedestal as once she held it in cultured, experienced, intelligent and cosmopolitan society. That is, the woman who has clung tenaciously to her virtue and

12

who has made a divinity of it. The virtuous heroines of fiction and the drama have today become
a laughing stock; readers and audiences decline
longer to take them seriously. And fiction and
drama are ever the mirrors of the thought and prejudice of the time. One speculates as to what it has
been that has brought about this revolutionary
philosophical somersault. What has caused the
man of today, contemplating holy wedlock, to be
more or less indifferent to his fair one's chastity?
What has caused women to change, as surely they
have changed, in their attitude toward virtue in
their own sex? What has converted physical purity
from an emblem of God into an emblem of the
slapstick? Let us guess at some of the under-
currents.

Although it is commonly assumed that virtue was
originally imposed upon women by men in order
that the security, dignity and self-esteem of the
latter might be duly safeguarded, it is much more
likely that virtue was originally imposed upon
women by women themselves, and for a simple
reason. Virtue was woman's sole protection against
other women. It was demanded by women of other

women because their men, as they knew all too well, were ever fetched by the unvirtuous woman and were weaned from them by her. Fearing such competition, women took every means to stave it off and destroy it by announcing the obloquy that they would make and did make the unvirtuous woman suffer. Now, it has long been a characteristic of woman that she has feared her sisters' opinion and estimate of her more than those of men, and the stratagem enjoyed, accordingly, its reign of prosperity. But, gradually, that prosperity grew less and less. For women began to find that it was no longer possible to attach obloquy to sexual dereliction in the way that they had once been successful in attaching it, since such dereliction had begun to take on a number of hitherto strange and disconcerting aspects which undermined and weakened the old stigma.

In the first place, there were ridiculous divorce laws which divorced, or at least separated, man and wife, while yet they did not actually divorce them. There were rulings as to various arbitrary periods, ranging up to three years, wherein the parties to the divorce, though they had already picked out their future mates, were forbidden to marry the latter. There were periods of from six months to a year that one of the parties had to spend in a certain State or otherwise endure until he or she obtained the desired release. There were utterly nonsensical barriers to marital dissolution that freed the parties yet didn't free them. The preponderant weight of public opinion was against all these legal devices. And, as a consequence, sexual dereliction by the separated parties with men and women denied legal union with them for the time being was quietly passed over. In the second place, obloquy is utterly ineffective and incapable of operation in the face of what is generally regarded as romance. Need I, at this tardy date, be guilty of observing again that the late war provided that romance, and in such bulk, in so far as the average man and woman were concerned, that all the old-maid moral opinion in the world was quite helpless against it? The girl whose affianced young man was about to go overseas, theoretically never to return, the nurse at the front with her charge apparently doomed to but a few more days of life, the lover on a fortnight's leave before going back into the slaughterhouse—the former order of stenciled morals disappeared in connection with such as these, and not only in the minds of those directly concerned but in the minds, or at least the hearts, of understanding and sympathetic outsiders. The bands were playing; the flags were streaming; the cannon were rumbling; the Sunday-schools were given over to Red Cross workers, sock-knitters and recruiting officers; the organs were playing not "Nearer, My God, to Thee," but "If He Can Fight Like He Can Love, Good-night Germany!" With two million men jumping at one another's throats, the chastity of some girl in Shamokin, Pa., seemed a negligible affair. And when at length the bands stopped playing and the flags no longer streamed and the cannon again were silent—and hundreds of thousands of men lay futilely dead under the soil—it seemed an even more negligible affair. That attitude has today not only not changed, it has grown stronger. A mother and father who have lost several sons in battle cannot be expected any longer to work themselves up to the same pitch of heartbreak that they once might have worked themselves up to over the mere loss of a daughter's virginity.

Physical chastity in women, for long regarded as an integral part of uprightness of character and of spiritual gentility and sweetness, is no longer so regarded. The old superstition that a woman who had sinned was hardened by the experience and morally, ethically and spiritually corrupted, has died out completely save in a narrow and unenlightened puritanical circle. The world, meditating the superstition, began to look the facts in the face. And the world was not long in finding out, if not always admitting the discovery openly, that, instead of hardening a woman, making her bitter and destroying her uprightness of character, a deviation from the straight path generally made her a better, finer and sweeter woman, one filled with a new understanding, a new gentleness and a new mercy. There were, the world found, tragedies, of course; there were on occasion sadness and despair and disaster. But for one such case there were a thousand of the other kind. And these other instances were hard—very hard, indeed,—to reconcile with the old meaning of sin.

It is entertaining, incidentally, in the light of the present attitude of the community toward sex, to consider the position of the various States in the Union in the matter of bigamy. In Alabama, the penalty for bigamy is from two to five years in prison, the penalty for forgery being, in the court's power, twice as many years. In Arizona, one may get not more than ten years for bigamy, but four more years for simple perjury. In Arkansas, a bigamist can get off with a three years' sentence, where he may have to serve fifteen years for perjury or twenty-one years for robbery. The same relative schedule obtains in many other States. In Louisiana, a bigamist faces the possibility of only a year in jail and a small fine, where a thief may have to serve fourteen years. In Maryland, the bigamist may get off with eighteen months, the very lowest sentence in the entire higher criminal catalogue of the State. In Nebraska, he need, in the court's discretion, serve only a year; in North Carolina, possibly only four months; in North Dakota, Ohio and Oregon, only a year; in South Carolina, only half a year; and in numerous other

States only a year. In Arkansas, on the other hand, the man who steals a mule may get fifteen years in the cooler and, in Texas, the stealing of a horse may bring a similar sentence.

That modern literature (both book and periodical), drama and even the cinema, in addition to reflecting the sex nonchalance of the period, have also directly influenced that nonchalance is more or less apparent. Three-quarters of the fiction and plays and a recognizable share of the motion pictures (for all we hear of censorship) presently view loose sex morals either lightly or romantically; gone almost entirely is the former uncompromising, tragic approach to the subject. The wages of sin is no longer death, but a happy ending. The little shopgirl's heroine is no longer the poor, abused virgin who, after years of hardship and misery, marries a kindly fellow of the neighborhood and settles down to a life of cottage firesides and babies, but a young woman in pink pajamas and a green hat who enjoys all the hazardous thrills of life and gets her husband in the end just the same as the more virtuous girl—and a very

19

much better one to boot. And what is true of Judy O'Grady is true also of the Colonel's lady's daughter.

§ 3

The War and Sex Morals.—The attributing of the present looseness of sex morals directly to the late war seems to me, however, to be for the most part inaccurate. While, as I have indicated, it is unquestionably true that the war inspired sexual nonchalance among women more or less directly concerned with it, such, for example, as volunteer nurses, young women resident within sound of the guns and others close to the actual scenes of conflict and to the participants therein, I doubt that the reasons assigned for the indifferent chastity of these quite cover the case of women further removed from the fighting countries. That the spirit of easy sex morals has animated these latter as well as their sisters, few will deny, for not in the memory of three generations has the world seen women so free in this respect as they are at present.

20

But if the war and the effects of the war are not responsible for the freedom, what is?

It is my opinion that the general Anglo-Saxon looseness in sex matters is the direct result of the more or less recent looseness in conversation, and that the latter, in turn, was the direct result not of the Freudian psycho-pathology, as some maintain, —not more than one person out of every ten thousand was even aware that such a man as Freud existed,—but the direct result of the wholesale influx into the English and American languages of fresh and lively slang words and phrases, many of which were synonyms for words and phrases which couldn't before be used in general conversation. It is possible to carry on a conversation today about many things that one couldn't mention ten years ago without being boxed on the ear or booted into the street. This has been brought about by the birth of the argot in point which makes possible the implication and expression of many things, most of them hitherto forbidden, without mentioning them by name. In addition, since the spirit of slang is a humorous one, the freedom in conversation

21

becomes doubly safe, since one may with impunity speak humorously where if one said precisely the same thing without humor one would be frowned upon. I thoroughly believe that, if there had been no war, we should have had the current sexual picnic just the same, and that slang would have been the responsible agent. It is slang that has broken down the former barriers of reserve; it is slang that has made quick intimacy possible; it is slang that has made a boy and girl feel at complete ease days and even months before they used to feel at complete ease with each other. Viewing the situation in America alone, we can't but face the fact that the speech of a generation ago was largely its own chaperon, whereas the speech of today is a quick-worker if ever there was one. Twenty years ago, after a young man had met a young woman at a party and had spoken with her for an hour or two, he asked her politely if he might call on her. Today, after a young man has met a young woman at a party, they know more about each other at the end of five minutes' conversation than their fathers or mothers will ever know.

§ 4

The New View of Sex.— The doctrine that there is a very considerable humor in sex, long upheld by the small minority of men and women who were able to think with their emotions, has spread so rapidly and so widely in the last decade that it is difficult to find more than one man or woman out of every dozen who doesn't currently believe in it. It used to be thought pretty generally that sex was a grim, serious and ominous business, to be entered into only by those duly joined in holy wedlock or by those lost souls already in thrall to the devil. Sex was synonymous with danger, tragedy, woe or, at its best, with legalized baby carriages. This view of sex has gone out of style with such other contemporary delusions as French altruism, the making of the world safe for democracy and the evil of Bolshevist government. I do not argue, plainly enough, that back in the cow pastures of the land the old view of sex does not still prevail, for it does; but wherever lights are brighter and there are paving stones and so much as a single electric street-car, wherever a band, however bad, plays on Saturday nights, there you will find a change in the old order. Sex, once wearing the tragic mask, wears now the mask of comedy. And whenever one laughs at a thing, one is no longer afraid of it.

I have alluded in the preceding paragraphs to the current prevalent looseness of conversation on sex matters. That conversation, as I have also indicated, generally takes on a humorous form, for one may be humorous about forbidden subjects with exemption, where a serious approach would be met with an offended air and rebuff. Many years ago, in my university days, I had a friend who played left end on the football team. It was my friend's technique—he was gifted with an irresistible talent for low comedy—to tell funny stories to the end playing opposite him on a rival eleven, weaken the latter with laughter and thus easily dispose of him. Since sex has become the playing-ground of conversational humor, we may believe that the technique of my football friend is often adopted in other directions.

What has brought about this view of sex as a humorous business is problematical. It is possible that the altered view has come about in due course of time and nature, that all such things move in inscrutable cycles and that once again we are in the midst of a quasi-Restoration turn of the clock. However, I make a guess in another direction. After a long and uninterrupted period of serious regard of anything, the wind always changes and there is born a sudden and recalcitrant laughter. Human nature is such that it cannot stand monotony; it demands relief. And history shows us that as surely as a period of high gaiety is followed abruptly by one of desolation and as surely as a period of misery is followed by one of prosperity, so, too, does a psychically and philosophically glum period inevitably soon or late give way to one of psychic and philosophical revelry. Thus, it is probable that the humorous view of sex has come about as a direct result of the long serious view of sex, that human nature simply demanded a change. As it deposed czars and kings and set up Yiddish pants-cutters and Wop soap-box ballyhoos in their places, so it deposed the tragedians and tragédiennes of sex and set up comedians and comédiennes.

But the change in the approach to the sex question has not, as might be inferred, been an arbitrary one. It is based upon a thoroughly clear and intelligent view of sex. Sex, in the great majority of instances, is a much more casual and unimportant thing than it is customarily admitted to be. An idiotic conspiracy has sought, with almost uniform success, to make the world accept it as something of paramount consequence in the life of man, the ground of his happiness or unhappiness, of his triumph or defeat, of his joy or his affliction. Yet the reflective man has long known that it is nothing of the kind, that it is, as a matter of fact, of considerably less importance in his general scheme of life than, say, his tobacco or his wine-cellar. Sex is, purely and simply, the diversion of man, a pastime for his leisure hours and, as such, on the same plane with his other pleasures. The civilized man knows little difference between his bottle of vintage champagne, his Corona Corona, his seat at the "Follies" and the gratification of his sex impulse. They all fall much under the same heading. He takes sex no whit more seriously than he takes, to put it superlatively, a symphony concert.

He sees in it simply something always amusing and sometimes beautiful, and lets it go at that.

Well, the world itself grows more and more civilized as century chases century down the alley of time and gradually it works itself up to the level of its more civilized inhabitants. And thus gradually the newer view of sex gains recruits. And what men believe, women in due time also believe. I do not say that such beliefs are commendable, for I am no judge, but merely an historian. I simply say that so long as men and women merely *felt* about sex, it was what it was yesterday. The moment they began instead to *think* about it, it dropped its mourning and wove vine leaves about its head—and painted its nose red.

In the course of man's contemplation of sex, one phenomenon has gradually impressed itself upon his consciousness above all others, and it is this one phenomenon that, more than anything else, has influenced him in his present attitude toward the subject. That sex is a relatively trivial and inconsequential event in life, that it is of infinitely less permanent significance in his scheme of things than his work in the world, however humble the nature of that work, or than his material welfare or his physical comfort or, as I have hinted, even certain other of his diversions, is clearly borne in upon him after a meditation of the history of sex life as it has directly concerned him.

One of the first things that strikes such a reflective man is the manner in which the brain cells themselves peculiarly operate to demote sex to a plane of unimportance. Such is the curious functioning of the male cerebral centres that the sex act, once it is so much as twenty-four hours past, quite passes from the memory or, at all events, from the direct consciousness. Although the fact, so far as I know, has never been articulated, it remains as an actuality that nothing is so quickly erased from masculine tablets of memory as the sex act accomplished. It is a mental idiosyncrasy, indeed, that the association of the act with a specific woman vanishes within an unbelievably short space of time, that so evanescent is the recollection that the woman actually seems a physical stranger to the man. What remains in the masculine mind is not the consciousness of the sex act, but only what may have proceeded from it, to wit, affection, companionship, friendship or spiritual, as opposed to physical, love. It is not an easy matter to set down delicately in type the almost incomprehensible degree to which this post-consciousness of sexual indulgence evaporates. Yet there is no man, if he will view himself honestly in the light of his experience, but will recall at once the peculiar sense of remoteness that has generally and quickly enveloped the woman with whom he has been on terms of physical intimacy. It would seem that nature, operating through the human mind, has contrived thus to make the world frequently a happier and more peaceful spot than it otherwise might be. In man's defective memory lies woman's symbol of chastity.

If sex were the important event in a man's life that some hold it to be, his mind would surely be influenced by it quite differently than it is. A woman, instead of so quickly and unintelligibly taking on the aspect of a complete physical stranger to him, would remain fixed in his sex consciousness. Sex would surely retain a vividness after its

29

performance that it actually does not retain. Yet, such is the baffling drollery of human nature that a man's wife ever seems to him a virgin.

§ 5

The Right-About-Face.—I have noted that the wide-spread change in sex morals that currently invites the attention of the professor of ethical biology is due, in part, to the increasing conviction that sex is not nearly the significant piece of Ibsenism that it long was held to be; that, in short, thinking men and women are coming to put the erstwhile emotional philosophy behind them and are substituting for it a sounder, more rational and vastly more workable understanding of the problem. But such a right-about-face does not just happen, Topsy-like; there are reasons for it. What are these reasons?

In the first place, modern men and women have found that it is utterly impossible to reconcile themselves to the theory that what gives them a natural emotional pleasure of the highest sort is validly synonymous with sin, or even that it is properly susceptible of social obloquy in the design of certain rococo laws. It is customary on the part of some persons to argue that if natural impulses of one sort are to be condoned, there is no reason why an indulgence in all kinds of natural impulses should not be privileged, and drug sellers, alcoholic drink peddlers, gambling-house operators and such like accordingly be duly licensed to practise their several callings. The taking of drugs and even the bibbing of ethyl alcohol are, however, not natural but acquired impulses, and no one but a fool would argue that the first is not a devastatingly evil and harmful thing or that the second, if too protractedly and greatly indulged in, is not also harmful to the individual and to society. There is sound reason at the bottom of the crusades against such things; the trouble with the crusade against rum is simply that it has been carried on in senseless terms of the crusade against drugs and so has made all intelligent persons laugh. Gambling, on the other hand, is a natural impulse, but it is not a natural impulse to wish to be cheated out of one's money by electrical wires, hidden mirrors, marked cards and confederates in the guise of head-waiters. And it is the duty of organized society to protect idiots from their own idiocy. In the case of sex, however, the intelligent person realizes that even the law at its harshest and most nonsensical makes sharp distinctions between these other deleterious forms of unnatural impulse and the natural impulse of sex, and that it holds sex expression in check only where it very definitely collides with personal or public interest. Sex indulgence *per se* is not under the ban of the law; only sex indulgence that directly opposes the welfare of society falls under that ban.

As for sin, well—there are many different opinions as to what constitutes sin and these many different conceptions and attitudes are obviously in full flower in a country like ours composed, as it is, of men and women of all the races of the earth, of all the religions of the earth, of all the various traditions of the earth and from the four corners of the world. In the State of Indiana, roller-skating has lately been declared a sin. In the State of Utah, cigarette smoking has officially been held to be a sin. In the city of Berkeley, California, it is considered a sin to play music on Sunday. It is a sin to shave on the Sabbath in Arizona or to pucker one's lips and whistle on the Sabbath in certain parts of the sovereign State of Massachusetts. It has at different times been declared a sin, by divers American sin-professors, to admire Zola, Rodin, Cabell and Anatole France. The stamp of sin, indeed, as we all know, has been placed upon such a plenitude of obvious innocences in the last twenty years that the word has, in the instance of most Americans outside of the Methodist churches, lost all accurate meaning. The travesty has gone so far that, today, actual sin, if there be such a thing, has suffered a loss of moral caste and has been snickered out of countenance with the ridiculously labeled sins that are not sins in any sense or degree. The result of this wholesale enunciation and cataloguing of sins, the result of denominating as wicked such completely innocent practices and diversions as dancing, playing cards, Sunday baseball, billiards, pool, prize-fighting and one-piece bathing suits, is the increasingly general conception of sexual pleasure as unsinful. The process of thought is here too readily comprehensible to call for explanation.

Into the moral philosophy of the American

melting pot there has been poured in multiplying measure the unpuritanical attitude toward sex of the various European, South American and Asiatic peoples who have become so considerably a part of us. These peoples have prospered amongst us and have become an increasingly dominant strain in the American blood. Four Americans out of every five have in them not only some of the blood of these aliens but, what is more, some of the processes of mind. And the stream of national morals has taken color from the foreign streams. Therefore, when we speak of American morality today we speak simply and to a very considerable degree of an alien morality that has been naturalized. This alien morality does not always recognize as sin what the earlier and more thoroughly native morality recognized as such. The Franco-American, the Italian-American, the Austro-American, the Hungarian-American, the Spanish-American, the Argentinian-American, the Cuban-American, the Armenian-American, the German-American and such like do not, out of the traditions of centuries, look upon sex exactly as the Puritan fathers did, and it is through the eyes of these that sex is more

34

and more being viewed by the growing generations of Americans.

To return to the opening key. More and more, too, is there evident amongst us a disposition to abandon the sex instruction of the young in the erstwhile bogie-man fashion and freely to admit to the adolescent mind—as Mrs. Mary Ware Dennett has expressed it in her intelligent essay, "The Sex Side of Life," addressed to her own and to other children—that sex has its share of thrill and joy. "Don't ever let any one drag you into nasty talk or thought about sex," she tells her children. "It is *not* a nasty subject. It should mean everything that is highest and best and happiest in human life. . . ." This emotional side of sex experience, wise parents have come to appreciate, can no longer conveniently be left out of the tutelage of the young. To leave it out is to begin the teaching of the alphabet of life with D. To leave it out is to send a youngster into the battle of life armed with a rifle that shoots backward at himself. And to believe, as some still believe, that such honest information honestly imparted to the young will tend to corrupt the latter is to believe that human

nature will still hide its wayward and ecstatic
secrets from them in their years to come.

§ 6

What Everybody Knows.—One of the most fetching ways in which to determine the altered contemplation of sex as it has developed amongst us
is to offer a glance to the various books on sex
which, up to a relatively short time ago, were sold
covertly in the small stationery and cigar stores
and which, for distribution through the United
States mails, were compelled to resort to the device
of the plain wrapper. I allude to such *opera* as
"What Every Boy Knows," "What Every Girl
Should Know," "What Every Married Woman
Should Know," "What Every Married Man Should
Know," "What Every Young Woman Should
Know" and "What Every Young Man Should
Know," together with such supplementary brochures as "Man's Sexual Life," "Woman's Sexual
Life," etc. Today, even the Government has taken
official cognizance of the changed attitude toward
sex, due to the almost universal enlightenment of
the public in the matter, and permits such books

freely to circulate through the post-office, secure in
the knowledge that what they contain is already
known to every American, male or female, young
or old, who can so much as read and that, further,
what is in them is to most of these so ancient a story
that they read it, if at all, merely for its archaic
humor. It is this wistful humor that accounts for the
prosperity that these books still enjoy. They are
perused by the young of the species no longer in the
secrecy of the attic or hayloft, as once they were, but
in the front parlor; and by the older folk they are
seized upon to be read aloud, for the delectation
of all connoisseurs of the rich and fruity, much
in the spirit of "Gentlemen Prefer Blondes" or a
French war report of 1916.

I have before me the various demi-tomes alluded
to. A study of them, in the light of the latter-day
attitude toward sex, fetches forth an illuminating
picture of the biological, ethical and sentimental
mind of 1927 as opposed to that same mind of
twenty or thirty years ago. Take, for example, the
volume entitled "What Every Married Man Should
Know." Therefrom, I cull such esoteric titbits as
these: 1. "The sacrificial ardor of motherhood for

the child is too well known to require elaboration";
2. "The sex urge must be handled rationally, with
common sense"; and 3, "Notwithstanding the pessi-
mism of those who see calamity in our present
divorce statistics, the modernist believes that not
only is there a more desirable and happy state in
the present sex relations between married couples,
but that there is a genuine progressive trend in
the direction of the monogamic ideal." That such
whangdoodle is believed by the adult male today,
that this mature mammal, who has laughed music
hall mother-ballads into the discard and who is
fully aware of the tremendous revenue currently
derived from women through the wide sale of birth
control devices, longer sentimentalizes the "sacrificial ardor of motherhood for the child," that he
longer believes that the sex urge personally or
generally is to be settled by logarithms, and that
he believes that the monogamic form of marriage
is showing a genuine progressive trend in the direction of an ideal—that he believes any or all of
such things is obviously ridiculous. He believes
nothing of the sort. For the sentimentalization of
motherhood, he wants the calm, clear and unroman-

tic truth. For the sex question, as it concerns himself, he wants not metaphysical hocus-pocus, but actual emotional experience and the discretion born thereof. Instead of a hymn to marriage, he wants a sharp, critical wallop on the bass-drum. He knows that marriage may increase spiritual love, but he knows full well that in actual operation it *de*creases physical love, or sex interest. And what he wants to know is what to do about it.

Back in the boll-weevil belt, there are, of course, married men who sleep with the family Bible in their undershirts and who still believe all that was told them at their grandfathers' knees; but for every one such there are a hundred men in other geographical centres who have some time since observed that grandpa's ideas, though very sweet and beautiful, somehow do not seem to work any more and who, accordingly, have been reduced to irreverent snickers. These men, looking back over their deplorable lives, have noticed that, for all their disobeying of grandpa's injunctions, the devil somehow hasn't got them yet, that sin, far from being its own punishment, has been rather jolly, and that men with long strings of letters after their names, who unquestionably know a great deal more about everything than they themselves know, have conclusively proved that it is as foolish to take the Bible literally as it is to take the New York *Graphic*. The result of their unholy meditations is not so much an open scoffing as a private conclusion to break the rules until they are caught. And the result of this conclusion, in turn, is that, to their pleasurable surprise and satisfaction, they find that they are seldom caught for the simple reason that every other fellow like them is so busy following his similar conclusion that he hasn't time to bother about anyone else.

If an apparent levity seems to insert itself into these observations, it is simply because the whole business has itself become enveloped in a measure of levity. The law is still the law; houschold morals are still household morals; honor, in so far as it ever existed in such matters, is still honor—and not only in the back reaches of the country but in the towns and cities as well. Yet the law and household morals and honor are one thing and human frailty is quite another. And when frailty becomes sufficiently general, it becomes its own court, its own judge and its own jury. If the 118,000,000 inhabitants of the United States were as one, at six o'clock sharp tonight, to enter each other's houses and steal the piano, piano-stealing would very shortly be endorsed and laughed out of the police courts. As sexual dereliction becomes more and more general, its erstwhile gray tone gradually takes on a lighter hue. If a pickpocket picking the pocket of a man in the Subway finds the latter simultaneously with his hand in *his* pocket, there's not much to be done about it.

In the book entitled "What Every Young Woman Should Know," I encounter this amazing philosophical cameo: "Adolescence and puberty are characterized by ill-defined longings; there are yearnings which account for the often rash nature of the adolescent; such newer movements as the Camp Fire Girls are doing a vast amount of good in giving this sex restlessness a constructive outlet." Imagine a young woman of today, assuming her to be other than a recently imported Swede chambermaid, believing that her sex impulses are to be satisfied by putting on a pair of khaki knickerbockers and sitting around a bonfire with a dozen

41

other girls discussing J. Fenimore Cooper and eating hot dogs! Plumbing the book further, we engage such things as the following: 1. "When a woman is cold to the marital advances of her husband . . . the state of affairs is highly conducive to unhappiness in the marriage relations and tends to disagreements, mutual dislike instead of love, and perhaps divorce"; 2. "By way of getting rid of certain sexual impulses, there are things the young woman can do. Take up a hobby whose interest will divert the mind: read good literature. There is plenty to be found in the lines of travel, biography and fiction"; 3. "To pursue their nefarious practices in greater safety and with increased profit, the shameless procurers of women carry on an *internationally organized* traffic—importing ignorant girls from Europe and elsewhere —not only to this country, but to all parts of the world, for the enforced practice of prostitution"; and 4. "Too often, an apparently innocent and kindly disposed invitation from an agreeable-mannered stranger has proven to be the mask for an ulterior purpose." The modern young woman, reading such stuff, either yawns or bursts out laughing. The book, recall, is addressed not to young girls—the latter are lectured to in a separate volume—but to fair ones between the ages of twenty-one and thirty.

It appears that among the unheard-of and amazing secrets that every married woman should be privy to are these: 1. "While it is true that sexual energy may to a large extent be diverted into other forms of expression, it is equally true that there is a point in the normal person's life beyond which this process cannot be carried without detriment to the individual. This is particularly true in the marriage state, where there are continual contact and sexual stimulations"; 2. "Coquetry, coyness and other feminine attributes are positive, if more or less subtle, evidences of sexual interest and expression. Many women excel in the active attraction of men, and by a subtle technique that is not by any means apathetic take the initiative in courtship"; 3. "By gentle, playful resistance and half-concealed attractions, the imagination is exercised and mutual desire originated, but a combative attitude should not be shown"; 4. "Happiness in marriage can only exist on a foundation of love, and love must be fostered and attended and not be taken for granted"; 5. "The fiery, impulsive, impetuous lover is often a selfish, vain, egotistical lover, and passion soon turns to ashes in the wake of his hectic course"; 6. "The wise wife will keep herself attractive and pay attention to the little details of person which mean so much to the lover, before marriage and after"; 7. "The problem of adjustments of temperament and other personal characteristics is an important one in marriage"; 8. "Intellectual growth depends upon ready exchange of ideas, reasoning and discussion, and nowhere is the open forum of free opinion more productive of valuable results than between a married couple"; 9. "Nagging has no place in the family circle of a modern marriage based on love"; and 10, and finally, "A sense of humor is perhaps the most essential thing in married life."

"What Every Boy Should Know" we find devoted largely to instruction in the sex life of plants and pollywogs. And "What Every Girl Should Know" to the important news that "A Chinese woman's foot is more interesting than her face to her husband, and no man of good breeding would look at a Chinese woman's foot in the street; such an act is most indelicate." Thus were the young of the species of yesteryear trained away, educated and safeguarded from the temptations of the flesh, the dangers of the *treponema pallidum,* and the future shadow of the divorce court!

§ 7

The Question of Economic Independence.—Among the leading reasons assigned for the altered status of sex is the increasing economic independence of women, with its consequently induced ethical autonomy. I hope that I shall not unduly offend the sensibilities of the professors when I observe that, though the reason has a share of truth in it, it has, in my estimation, a considerably greater share of buncombe. What economic independence unquestionably induces in a woman is, true enough, a relative indifference to the hitherto feared opinion of those upon whom she was directly dependent, but what it simultaneously induces—and the professors seem conveniently to overlook the fact —is an of necessity increased and vastly more important regard for the opinion of those upon

45

whom her new-found economical independence and all the comfort and happiness it carries with it are in turn dependent. It is today twice as necessary for the woman in the professions or in trade to be careful of her reputation as it is for her sister who leads what may generally, if unsatisfactorily, be described as a private or home life. For every "æsthetic" dancer or movie actress or lady novelist or Maeterlinck trouper who allows her wicked will a free functioning, there are a score who have to watch their steps with considerably more care than the ex-débutante, the miller's daughter or the pastor's wife. If they do not, their contracts, under the new dispensation, may be annuled, or they may, as in a recent lamentable instance, have their profitable lecture engagments canceled by the Babbitts, or they may find themselves, as in another recent and equally lamentable instance, laughed off the platform into the vestibule. The woman in trade must be even more circumspect than the one in the arts and professions. The woman in business has her boss and the prejudices of her boss, often hypocritical, to bear in mind. Even the lowly upstairs maid who carries on with the chauffeur or

46

with the son of the household when he is home from Princeton will be promptly booted out into the street, and she knows it. The increasing economic independence of women, whether considerable or relatively puny, tends coincidentally to increase women's wariness in the matter of sexual indulgence. The theory that it does not is, like so much of the current sex philosophy, simply a theory.

But the fact remains, nonetheless, that the sex freedom is here. That one fact, such as that noted above, collides with the other and greater fact no more gets rid of the second fact than the collision of a trolley car with the Twentieth Century Limited gets rid of the latter. The economically independent woman is not sex-free because of her economic independence, but in spite of it. Because of it, she must have recourse to concealments and stratagems that other women need resort to in a lesser degree.

§ 8

In the Colleges.—Just as straws show which way the wind blows, so do equally little things show which way the youth of the land blows. As symptoms of the changed attitude of American young men toward young women, and *vice versa*, I quote a few recent sample pleasantries from various undergraduate college humorous journals:

a.

He: You certainly are a nice girl.

She: Yes—but I'm getting damned tired of it!

b.

Say, girlie, are you very fast?

Listen, boy, give me five minutes with a man and he's a fellow with a past.

c.

She entered the sorority house a pure, innocent angel; she came out a woman.

d.

Little Boy No. 1: Hey, Johnny, let's play college. I can get overalls and a pipe.

Little Boy No. 2: But all the girls we know are decent.

e.

If at first you don't succeed, remember that all co-eds aren't the same.

f.

What would any Christian woman be doing out this late at night in a closed car?

The same thing a heathen woman would.

g.

A college boy is one who knows what she wants when she wants it.

48

h.

John calls his machine "Estimation."
What's the point?
So many girls have fallen in it.

i.

Do you believe in marriage?
Only as a last resort.

j.

The modern co-ed is defined as one who has a shotgun in her
hope-chest.

k.

A miss is as good as a mile. Any farther away than that you
can take a chance that she may not want to walk back.

The quotations are from college papers extending from Harvard on the East to Leland Stanford on the West. Fifteen years ago or even less, if the editors of the college journals had dared to print such jokes, the outraged faculties would have hauled them onto the carpet instanter. Today they are printed as a matter of course.

§ 9

The Mystery of Sex.—One of the drollest phrases ever concocted by mortal man is "the mystery of sex." Save in the instance of boys and girls under

49

the age of sixteen or thereabout (in the country districts the age limit is one or two years lower), there is no more mystery to sex than there is to an amateur card trick. The average boy and girl of eighteen in this enlightened and realistic age know almost all there is to know about sex (in the accepted sense of the word), if not by actual experience, at least by vicarious experience, and it is no more mysterious to them than their breakfast oatmeal. True enough, they contribute to the life of the delusion by professing a surprise at and ignorance of the matter in order to safeguard their parents from concern and their seats from wallops, but any man or woman who will reflect upon his or her young years knows that sex was, if not an open book, at least an open pamphlet to him or her long before he or she permitted anyone else to suspect the fact.

What is called the mystery of sex is really not concerned with sex at all, or at least in very small part; the mystery is that of personality. It is not sex that causes half the trouble of the world, but the deviousness and provocation of personality. To say that the average man is attracted to the average woman by the mystery of sex is the sheerest sort of drivel. The average man is attracted to the average woman, and *vice versa,* by the thrill of a comely face, the charm of a bag of tricks, the challenge to preposterous vanity—one or more of a half dozen such things. Sex has very little to do with it, except in the instance of actors, barbers, sailors and other such often mythical guinea pigs, none of whom, incidentally, by any stretch of the imagination may be said to regard sex precisely as being very mysterious. Sex, to the more civilized man or woman, is a too familiar business longer to hold out any overpowering curiosity. From a matter of the first importance it soon descends to a matter of secondary importance. Its romance, so to speak, generally fades contemporaneously with the age at which the romance of "A Prisoner of Zenda" and novels of a piece begins to seem just a trifle nonsensical. And with the evaporation of sex's mystery and the subsequent diminution of its romantic aspect, man and woman, ever desirous of prestoing themselves into a captivating illusion of one sort or another, begin to look around them for new materials of delusion. These materials

51

they find in one another's looks, manners, thoughts, clothes, tastes, and what not—in short, in one another's personalities. Around these personalities they weave the mystery and romance that have ceased to enwrap sex some time since.

To argue, as is argued, that the sex impulse is nevertheless at the bottom of this personality attraction is, I believe, to argue a fallacy. It is true, of course, that sex lies at the end of the road, that it constitutes the third act of the personality attraction, so to speak; but, unless I am peculiarly in error, it is infinitely less deliberate and infinitely more casual than is commonly maintained, chiefly by biologically stale gentlemen who offer contradiction by way of persuading others that they are still in the ring. The average civilized man, some of our leading novelists excepted, thinks of sex only in off moments. He has tried it often enough to know that there is three times more excitement in an airplane flight and ten times more pleasurable satisfaction in a bottle of Dry Imperial 1906, or, for that matter, even 1911. He knows that it is occasionally amusing, as a burlesque show, a negro ball or a debate in the Senate is amusing, but he knows at the same time that the humor, the gentleness, the nonsense and the charm that is woman is, compared with her sex, as greatly superior in amusement power as is the "Bauern Cantate" to the "Trauerode." The so-called mystery of sex has produced the novels of Elinor Glyn and the songs of Tin-Pan Alley. The explicitness and obviousness of sex have produced the novels of all the first-rate artists that the world has known, and the music of Richard Strauss.

§ 10

Monogamy.—The success of the monogamic institution of marriage in these later days of Caucasian civilization must be looked for very largely outside the cities and in the small towns, villages, farms and other such places where life is relatively drab and uneventful. Where life is thus drab and uneventful, monogamy flourishes, as the cactus flourishes best in a desert. Its very irritations, annoyances, disgusts, plate-throwings and even fist-fights are the things that perpetuate it, since they, distasteful as they are, yet offer themselves as compensatory fillips in the miserable humdrum of life immediately beyond the household walls. It is impossible to imagine the failure of a marriage on a deserted island; it is almost as difficult to imagine the failure of a marriage in a settlement of five hundred or a thousand people where there isn't even a movie parlor, where the railroad-crossing man's mother-in-law is the only suspect houri within twenty miles—and where the roads are bad—, and where any person who doesn't go to bed with the cows is given a hard look by the pastor on Sunday morning. It is obvious that a marriage disintegrates less frequently from internal than from external causes. Thousands of married couples who hate the sight of each other and would give their last nickel to mash the breakfast grapefruit against each other's noses stay married nevertheless, and so contribute their mite to the delusion, shared by the less reflective statistician, that monogamy is a success. But the moment a husband lays an eye on a woman who coddles his fancy and causes him to lament the fact that his wife's hair is black instead of yellow, or the moment a wife begins to take too great an interest in fortune-telling or quotes at the dinner table the charming remark passed to her by her osteopath, that moment does a shyster lawyer somewhere begin figuring on buying a new body for his Buick. In the cities, these deplorable external critiques of monogamous marriage are plenteous; in the rural regions, they hardly exist.

The married yokel looks about him and sees that his married lot is no worse than that of his neighbor's. If his wife needs a good shampoo and garters to keep her cotton stockings from looking like exhausted accordions, so does his neighbor's wife and that neighbor's wife in turn. If the corned beef and cabbage his own wife cooks for him tastes like a valise boiled in wall-paper, the corned beef and cabbage that wafts into his window from the house across the mule path smells as if it would taste the same. If the physical appeal of his spouse is approximately as strong as that of an old cigarette picture of Lydia Thompson, so is that of every other squaw in the reservation. So he simply sits back, heaves a sigh and waits patiently for a blonde angel in a white nightie in the hereafter. The city man, on the other hand, suffers a matrimonial doubt almost every time he looks out of the window or walks down the street on a windy day. And so, also, does his wife. For every marriage that is dissolved for statutory reasons there are ten that begin to wobble toward disintegration simply because a husband quite innocently, but unforgettably, likes the way in which his secretary smiles good-morning at him or because a wife admires the way in which some other fellow of her acquaintance keeps his trousers up without suspenders.

§ 11

Why Men Marry.—Not long ago, there were gathered together in one of the esoteric *salles à boire* of New York, a dozen middle-aged men. All save two were benedicks. As the mineral water began to work its magic on those at the board, the two bachelors bade of their fellows to tell them honestly the reasons that had prompted them to marry the women they had married. What, in other words, precisely had it been about these women that had fetched the men and converted them into husbands? The ten husbands pondered the question gravely and then, in turn, gave out the underlying provocative causes, which I set down seriatim:

56

1. Because the woman had shared a taste for F. W. Bain's translations of the Hindu "Digit of the Moon" and "Bubbles of the Foam," could play the piano, and had Japanese eyes.

2. Because the woman disliked public restaurants and jazz music, and liked to stay home at nights.

3. Because the woman had a beautiful soft speaking voice and hated golf and all golf players.

4. Because the man had been thrown over by the woman he really loved.

5. Because the woman had $50,000 in the bank which the man needed to buy a partnership in the firm for which he was working.

6. Because the woman dressed in a way the man admired; because she hadn't bobbed her hair; and because she shared the man's wish to make a trip to Cairo.

7. Because the man was tired of living at his club and because he felt that he was getting old.

8. Because the woman had been attentive to him during an illness of two months' duration.

9. Because the woman had an even temper; be-

cause she spoke three languages fluently; and because she was the only woman the man had ever
met who didn't wear her fingernails sharply pointed
like a Chinaman's.

10. Because she was the best-looking girl at the
resort where the man spent his Summers.

Although these may at first glance seem to be
excessively superficial reasons for the men's
marrying the respective women, I thoroughly believe that they represent accurately the basic reasons that often shove men into the state of hyme-
neal blessedness. It is upon such a profound philosophical basis that the great institution of marriage
is frequently founded; it is upon such a basis that
the lions and unicorns of genealogy proudly prance
and lift their heads to Heaven.

§ 12

Intellectuality and Sex.—One of the oldest themes
in our literature concerns the impossibility of a
merely intellectual union between a man and a
woman, at least one of whom is comparatively
young and possessed of the tremors that go with

youth. Of the soundness of the theme, there is not
the slightest doubt; yet one or two issues related
to it are generally overlooked by its confectioners.
The civilized woman, it is true, has no use for a
man of even the most transcendent intellect if sex
is no part of him. But, on the other hand, the same
woman has equally small use for a man of even the
most transcendent sex if intellect is no part of him.
That intellect, surely enough, may actually be of
a not much higher level than that of a congressman
or a gas-bill collector, but this is not the point.
Whatever its bulk, it must pass for intellectuality
with the woman; she must believe in it and take
it for granted, as she believes in and takes for
granted her God, her baby's beauty and the security of her garters. The man may, in good sooth,
be an unmitigated ass, but not to her. Back of her
husband's amatory virtuosity, a wife must discern
a compendium of learning and worldly wisdom
that, in her mind, puts Socrates to the blush. If
she doesn't feel in her sub-conscious that her husband is a sapient fellow, he had better begin to
keep a sharp eye on the iceman.

§ 13

The American Home.—One of the phenomena that entertains the spectator of the present-day American scene is the gradual but unmistakable disruption and disappearance of American home life. Not only in the larger cities is it increasingly manifest that the home life of even a generation ago is no more, but in the smaller towns, as well, is the decline evident in a relative degree. To this simple fact, I believe, are attributable most of the theoretically complex ills which afflict the modern American morality: increasing marital dissatisfaction, sexual promiscuity, divorce, looseness and cheapness of taste, general unrest and discontent, and the various allied corruptions of society and the spirit. It may be a banality that a man's four walls are his fortress against unhappiness, but it is none the less true. That way lies human nature. Once let a hole be shot through them, and the pikes of the enemy may be clearly seen drawing near.

Up to a generation ago, the American home, both in the cities and smaller places, was more or less inviolate and intact. There were few agencies operating against it. Today such agencies have been increased fifty-fold, with the result, plain even to a blind man, that the average American home is no longer a harbor and a haven but rather a mere place of debarkation. The married man, his wife and his children no longer see their home as a retreat and a safeguard from the world, but as a dressing-room in which to make up for the show on the outer stage. And even where they do not so see it, they see it as a place not of peace and rest and homely quiet but as one to be made indistinguishable from a sideshow. The object of most Americans today is not to remember that their home is a home, as the home of their fathers and mothers was, but to forget that it is one. As instruments toward this to them soothing forgetfulness they have recourse to any number of things of which their fathers and mothers knew nothing and which contribute to the converting of the old-time fireside into a pyrotechnical display. Thus, where once a family gathered in quiet to hold converse or to read, where once the boys and girls learned to play the piano, where once there hovered over a home the intangible but indelible mist-blanket of contentment and heart's-ease, today all is noise, nervousness and excitement from without. The radio and the phonograph are brought in to retail prize-fights and the latest monkeyshines of Memphis niggers. Cheap automobiles bring a score of intruders where once difficult modes of transportation made callers rare. Cheap telephones banish privacy and bring the outside world, with its temptations, close to the door. Where, once, going to the theatre was an event, for there was, among other things, the expense to be considered, cheap movies have now made such pleasure-going a nightly possibility. Young boys and girls twenty years ago thought of dancing only on relatively rare and gala party occasions; today, the phonograph and radio make it an easy and common indulgence. In the cities, too, there are hundreds of dance places calling where formerly there were none; in the little towns there are the ice-cream parlors and roller-skating rinks with their mechanical pianos.

Such things, and the others that they suggest, may seem trivial, but that, in combination, they have broken up the old American home life is readily perceptible. The girl who has danced so much as once in a brilliantly illuminated and gilt-smeared public hall does not look at the walls of her home in quite the way she did before. The man whose home, when his day's work is over, is—even though it be of his own making—a radio lecture bureau and jazz factory is not a man with tranquillity in his heart. A woman with a telephone constantly at her ear is a woman first and a wife and mother second. Show me an American home with a radio called upon to entertain it, with children abandoning their playing of "The Beautiful Blue Danube" on the piano to do the Black Bottom in front of a phonograph, with pictures of Pola Negri and John Gilbert above the kitchen sink, with the telephone ringing and with a Ford at the front door, and I'll show you a family that is heading rapidly for trouble.

§ 14

The Moralist.—Morality is a species of disease, of weakness. The completely healthy man is never a moralist. There never has been a moralist who hasn't suffered—and hasn't personally been aware of the disturbing fact—from a physical deficiency in a certain unmentionable direction.

THE AMERICAN EMOTION

§ 1

Emotional Stimuli.—The observer of the emotional reactions of the American people is brought to the lamentable conclusion that the stimuli which produce those reactions most magnificently show a constantly increasing cheapness and standardization. The American of today responds to a multiplicity of emotional spurs that, in the aggregate, are the most puerile and stereotyped in Christendom, a fact duly noted by the men who make their livings and reputations off his psychical responses. To persuade the American to react positively to these various magnets is a simple matter; he takes to them as a duck to water.

Consider, for example, the means whereby he is readily brought to an admiration of whichever politician desires his esteem. Privy to the secrets of his emotional gullibility, the politician who wishes to woo his good-will sets about securing it in the following rubber-stamp manner: first, by having his photograph taken with his wife; second, by having his photograph taken with his wife and children; third, by having his photograph taken with his old mother; fourth—and best, if possible —by having his photograph taken with one or both of his grandparents, a view which is invincible in convincing the American that the fellow, no matter whether his grandparents were horse-thieves, comes of solid stock; fifth, by getting his name on the boards of charitable organizations, even though he never once shows up at board meetings; sixth, by patting newsboys genially on the head in public places, thus attesting to his humanness and democratic nature; seventh, by wearing clothes of a not too recent cut, and so indicating that he is one of the plain people; eighth, by pitching his voice an octave lower than is natural, thus giving himself the necessary he-man aspect; ninth, by never making a speech on any occasion save the Fourth of July or a fraternal organization conclave without much profound frowning; tenth, by alluding on every possible public occasion to the humbleness of the folk from which he sprang; eleventh, by mopping his brow as much as possible when facing an audience, by way of subtly flattering inference that he is hard put to it to convince so august an assemblage of minds; twelfth, by approaching a movie news reel camera in a slightly hesitating and diffident manner, as if he did not deem himself worthy of so great an honor; thirteenth, by wearing a silk hat only at Easter; fourteenth, by affecting a deep interest in baseball; fifteenth, by never smoking cigarettes in a holder, an act which would bring him to be viewed as a fancy fellow and one to be looked on with certain misgivings; sixteenth, by wearing a collar that doesn't fit him and which thus somewhat occultly persuades the American to regard him as a man so busy with important concerns that he has no time for such trivial details; seventeenth, if the owner of an automobile, by having one of a not too expensive or fashionable make and by making sure that it is of no color other than black; eighteenth, if a college man, by attending more laboring-men's balls and picnics than would otherwise be necessary; nineteenth, by never failing to have

Thanksgiving dinner with his family; and twentieth, by denouncing his opponent before election day as being everything from a rat to a skunk, and after election day, whether he is elected or defeated, by admitting generously that, after all, his opponent is a very fine fellow indeed.

Not less incomplex than the hocus of the politician in cajoling a satisfactory emotional response out of his countrymen is that ever successfully put into operation by the impresarios of public band concerts, movie house orchestras and other such musical *coups de grâce.* Four facts are closely borne in mind in such cases: first, that the American will invariably respond to anything of a military or patriotic nature, even though it reflect, like Tschaikowski's 1812 overture, alien excitements; second, that he will uniformly be moved by obvious musical sentimentality; third, that either unusually rapid or become-standardized "devout" music will fetch him the one way or the other; and fourth, that he will ever regularly be brought to a high emotional tension and consequent applause by any composition that works crescendo up to a boiler-factory finale with drums and brass raising a hell of a racket. Thus, at every such impresario's hand there is a catalogue of sure-fire numbers, ready at a moment's notice to jounce the American in this manner or that. The list includes such compositions as the following: "Medley of National Airs," Nevin's "Narcissus," Wagner's Pilgrims' Chorus, Mendelssohn's "Spring Song," Brahms' Hungarian Dances, Nos. 6 and 7, Tobani's "Hearts and Flowers," Tosti's "Good-bye," Chopin's Nocturne in E flat major, Dvořák's "Humoreske," Sousa's "Stars and Stripes Forever," Verdi's "Stabat Mater," Liszt's Second Hungarian Rhapsody, Tschaikowski's "Pathétique," the slow movement of Chopin's B flat minor sonata, the Meditation from "Thaïs," Nevin's "The Rosary," the intermezzo from "Cavalleria Rusticana," the "Flower Song" from "Faust," Weber's "Der Freischütz," "Silver Threads Among the Gold," Elgar's "Salute d'Amour" and the "Poet and Peasant" overture. It matters not how often these be repeated, the evocation of emotional response is always certain, and always to be placed in a definitely labeled pigeon-hole. Thus, the inevitable reaction to such a tune as "Dixie" is not due to its patriotic nature or to its sentimental associations—for the reaction is registered among the many Americans of the North as of the South—but rather, as the wily impresarios are aware, to its rapid and hence superficially stimulating movement. Thus, again, the reaction to "Der Freischütz" is not grounded upon any quality that the work possesses, but to the din it makes. And thus, still further, the popular response to the MM. Tosti, Nevin and Tobani is allied to precisely the same species of psychic vibrations as are set into motion by such analogous stimuli as dolorously orchestrated magazine stories about poor working girls and dogs.

It is a well-known psychological laboratory experiment that proves that a mutt may be made to howl melancholiously when certain notes are sounded upon an amplified zither or when certain chords are played upon a regulation piano. It is a perhaps less well-known experiment that testifies that the average American may be made to feel a pleasantly permeating melancholy when much the same chords are played upon a piano. I am here not guilty of offensive statement, as some may imagine. The test may readily be made and its truth as simply established. Go down into the street, gather together the first half dozen Americans you can find there, fetch them back into a room, and play *dolentemente* these chords: *f-sharp, c, e; d, g-sharp, c;* and *e, g-sharp, c, e*—or some such arpeggio as *c, b-flat, f-sharp, a.* And note the result.

* * *

That mere gaudiness is the strongest bait for the American's æsthetic admiration is surely not news, but the ways in which it operates are perhaps not generally recognized. The figures of the Woolworth and Kresge chains of five and ten cent stores show that, in any one of the last seven years, it has always been the articles of loudest color or fanciest aspect, regardless of their intrinsic utility, which have enjoyed the largest and steadiest sale. The figures of the theatrical booking offices show similarly that, in three cases out of five, the play that is housed in a road theatre whose lobby electrical illumination is the brightest generally draws a better business than the play, whatever its quality, that is housed in a less externally enticing theatre. In the instance of moving picture theatres, it is the biggest and most showy theatre that gets the steadiest regular draw, regardless of the quality of films displayed therein—as, for example, the Capitol or Paramount or Roxy in New York. In the way of architecture, the taste is for any structure whose façade is idiotically suffused at night with the so-called hidden-light device. In this connection, ask any visitor to New York, for example, which building of all the buildings in the city he has most admired and most clearly remembers and the odds are ten to one that he will say the American Radiator Building, once appropriately described by a metropolitan wit as Gloria Swanson's town-house. If a pleasure-park is not painted in startling colors, it is sure to lose money. Thus, Luna Park, with its brilliant scarlets, is still going, whereas the old Dreamland, across the way, and smeared with a less dazzling hue, lost money and went into the discard long before the elements of nature finished it off completely.

Ever since Barnum wisely and auspiciously figured out that the gaudy poster would invariably fetch the biggest crowds into the tent before which it was hung, not less sagacious showmen, merchants and caterers to the public taste generally have followed the principle he inaugurated. Beeman's sedate black and white chewing gum package thus lost ground to Wrigley's flashy cerise and green package; magazines with lack-lustre saffron covers had to obey the Barnum philosophy and go in for flashing scarlets and pinks and golds; book jackets that once were generally white are now all the colors of the rainbow; of all the soaps of yesterday the one that has survived most successfully is Sapolio with its silver and blue circus wrapper; the haberdashers' reports indicate that, for all the obscene jokes cracked against them, more red neckties are sold annually than any others; where the "ready-made" tailors used to sell more blue suits than suits of any other color, they presently sell more light grays, greens and conspicuous browns; twenty years ago, when the American bought a soft hat, he bought a black one—today he goes in for fawn-colored, tan, brown, green, pearl gray and three or four other shades; clerks used always to wear black bands on their straw hats—today they wear bands of all the colors in the spectrum; candy merchants used to put up their wares in plain white boxes with now and again some gilt lettering on the top—if they wish to do any business today they must put them up in boxes that look like delirium tremens, otherwise they will lose their custom to their nearest competitor. And so it goes in all departments of American life and trade.

*   *   *

Returning more directly to the subject of emotional reaction, let us consider the American in relation to the art of poetry. The managing director of one of the largest newspaper syndicates in the country informs me that, after fifteen years of experiment with newspaper verse, he has found that the most popular type of "poetry" is that written for him by a woman with utterly no sense of genuine poetic beauty and that deals in the most elementary manner possible with these ten themes; (1) a dying dog; (2) mother; (3) longing for a lost love; (4) the joy of a Spring day; (5) baby's toes; (6) the house in which one was born; (7) hills with snow on them; (8) sailing on a lake of blue; (9) the moon shining on water; and (10) anything about pine trees. Any verse dealing with one of these subjects is certain of much commendatory letter-writing, it appears, where verse treating of anything else, however finely wrought, evokes nothing but a blank and evidently distasteful silence. In the matter of boiler-plate cuts or illustrations, the four most popular, for the period extending from January 1, 1924, to January 1, 1927, were, the statistics demonstrate, pictures exhibiting a baby smiling and reaching out its arms; a young man seated on a bench in the moonlight holding hands with a young woman; a child patting a large dog, with the caption "Comrades"; and a woman playing a harp with angels hovering above.

In the direction of fiction, this same syndicate, which pretty well covers the country, experimented for three years with stories by the better literary craftsmen, either published for the first time or in second serialization. The experiment was a complete failure; the American public outside of one or two of the larger cities would have nothing of them. The syndicate manager, properly appreciating that literary quality was a handicap rather than an asset and that what the nation in the aggregate wanted were emotionally stimulating plots, however crudely told, then assembled a company of hacks to turn out such daily short stories as would capture the American heart and fancy. Success was now his reward. For the last eight years the country has gobbled up these stories as a rat gobbles up cheese. Just as we have statistics on the species of verse and illustrations, so have we statistics on the favorite story themes. These themes are so popular, in point of fact, that they may each be repeated no less than five times a month. The eight subjects which best cull the American heart-throb are, in the order named, discovered to be the following: (1) the return of a long-lost son on his mother's birthday; (2) the saving of a child, at the point of death, by a mother's night-long prayers, the recovery coming as dawn is breaking; (3) the return of a boy believed to have been killed in the war and his mating with his faithful sweetheart, the little girl next door; (4) the lovers separated years before who meet again in old age and marry; (5) the story about a humble woodsman who turns out in the last sentence to be Abraham Lincoln; (6) the girl who is coveted by a villain and who humbles him into uprightness of character by telling him of her dead mother and playing "Lead, Kindly Light" on the piano; (7) the brutal husband who is brought to mend his ways and tearfully beg his wife's forgiveness when their only child is run over in the street below the tenement and killed; and (8) the old G. A. R. veteran who goes to the cemetery on Decoration Day and places a wreath on the grave of his son killed in the late war.

§ 2

Emotional Hypocrisy.—The outstanding hypocrisy of the American is his reaction to emotion. Ashamed of his own emotions, at least in what may be called their finer shadings, he seeks to conceal his true nature by scoffing loudly at any display of such emotions on the part of one of his less hypocritical compatriots. He doesn't hesitate duly to cry copiously over the predicament of some absurd heroine of some absurd theatrical exhibit, or duly to laugh broadly over the humorous embarrassments of some hero of fiction, or duly to yell himself hoarse when a band tunes up on "Columbia, The Gem of the Ocean," or duly to cheer any gent in an American military uniform when the said gent's image is reflected on a movie screen, or duly to bestow an affectionate smack upon his twins at bedtime, or duly to take his wife to dinner at Childs' on their wedding anniversary, or duly to hit a man in the nose if the fellow makes a derogatory remark about his mother, or duly to get up and give his seat in a street-car to an old, gray-haired woman with one leg. In such junctures he permits his emotions to enjoy full play, and is proud of the permission he vouchsafes them. But in the case of any emotion of a somewhat more delicate and exotic tint, he conducts himself much like a small boy who has been kissed by the school-teacher and who, desirous of impressing the other boys that, for all that, he isn't a sissy, fingers his nose at the teacher immediately she turns her back.

In the view of the American, there is something unmanly in a display of any emotion between the sexes or, in fact, of any emotion not commonly and publicly shared and indulged in by the man in the street. This accounts for the American's voracious relish of marital, divorce and other such journalistic scandals and, as a corollary, the length to which sagacious newspaper editors go in the retailing of them. It accounts, too, for the recent tremendous success of the tabloid journals, which are built entirely upon the principle of holding up to scorn any citizen who has indiscreetly allowed his emotions a free course and thus converted himself into a laughing-stock for all pew-holders, members of the Y. W. C. A. and bloomer salesmen. Nothing induces in the American such an elaborate series of camouflaging winks and wise-cracks as a fellow patriot's marriage with a young and too good-looking blonde, an unrestrained love letter, a man blackmailed under the Mann Act, an elopement after a gin party, an amorous dereliction from the code of Increase Mather, a romance unintelligible to a paperhanger, the spectacle of a couple of lovers on a park bench, the late Autumn moon, or a first-rate poet.

§ 3

Persuading the American.—Professors of the native popular psychology have long recognized the fact that the American is seldom to be persuaded of a given thing directly, and that, if he is to be won over to one or another point of view, the job must be done in an oblique manner. A glance at several recent popular American convictions substantiates the verity of the professors' findings. Prohibition was sold to the American people not by telling them plainly and directly that alcoholic liquor was bad for them, which they would have resented as an insult to their own powers of self-control, but by telling them discreetly and flatteringly that it was bad for persons who had no self-control. The late war was sold not by telling the people that Germany was an enemy but by telling them that France was a friend. Coolidge sold himself not by talking common-sense but by refraining from talking nonsense. Nine-tenths of the Americans who presently believe in evolution do not believe in it because they have been told it is a scientific fact, but simply because they have

80

been made to laugh at its funny-looking opponents.

§ 4

The American Reaction.—To the phenomena of life which surround him, the American responds with clock-like precision in one of two ways, to wit, on the one hand, with an *Hooray!* or, on the other, with a *Go-to-hell!*

THE MOTHERLAND

§ 1

The American Attitude Toward England.—Let us look at the facts squarely, and undeluded by the cheap sateen hypocrisies of ward-politician diplomatists. Let us get rid of all this assuaging bosh about the bond of a common language, about mutual interest and about identity of blood and race that is trotted out to lullaby the issue at Anglo-American banquets at the Cecil Hotel, at Seamen's Fund concerts aboard the ocean liners and at Bankers' Club lunches to visiting British profiteers. A common language didn't hold up the Wars of 1775 and 1812; identity of blood and race didn't forestall the American Civil War, nor prevent the Anglo-Saxon English from siding with its participants of French, Spanish and Creole descent; mutual interest, if it were more than so many words, wouldn't have made it necessary for Grover Cleveland to pass his celebrated remark to England in the matter of Venezuela. We can get nowhere by resorting to the subterfuge of such comfortable and meaningless phrases; we must look behind them. Thus looking, what do we discover?

Soothing handclasps and quasi-secret fraternal grips aside, we discover that England and America are farther apart today than they have been since 1895. On the surface, the appearance is otherwise, but, below, the undertow is plainly to be felt. In the first place, the interests of the two nations are fast pulling in different directions. Where, for instance, would the interest of England lie in the event of war between the United States and Japan? Where, again, would the interest of the United States lie in the event of war between England and the new Germany? As for identity of blood and race, the identity is presently less than it has ever been in the history of America; the Anglo-Saxon blood stream in the United States has been declining steadily with the passing of the years; it gives ground gradually but surely to the infiltration of middle-European, south-European and Asiatic strains. And as for a common language, all that the English optimist need do to disillusion himself

is to come over here, get on a train and make stop-
overs in the Pennsylvania Dutch region, the German areas of the Northwest, the Swiss colonies of
the Pacific Coast, the Italian and Czech settlements
in the mining States, the French and Spanish
stretches along the Gulf, the Slav colonies along
the North Atlantic seaboard, the Scandinavian
areas of the middle Northwest and the scattered
Negro belts, to say nothing of the New York East
Side, the Dakota prairies and the Southwestern
frontier States. But beyond all this there is something else, something much more important, and
that is the notion, inculcated in every American
schoolboy for more than a century, that the two
nations are natural enemies. Ask any little American boy today who has got through his primary
school history and who didn't have an older brother
killed in the late war which he would rather fight
against, England or Germany, and the youngster
will select England. They may alter the school-
books all they care to, but they can't alter the fact
in the little boy's mind that his George Washington
fought the English, that his John Paul Jones fought
the English, that the English bribed Benedict

Arnold to betray his country and that every Fourth of July firecracker is a red-coated soldier of George III to be blown to kingdom come.

It is a characteristic of the American that he is very cocky, provided the odds are overwhelmingly in his own favor, and, accordingly, as all these little boys grow to manhood and find that the United States is tremendously the superior of Great Britain in wealth, man power, petrol resources (important to modern warfare), etc., it is not unnatural that they should desire once again to match strength with the ancient enemy. For we must remember that the majority of these boys now grown up are typical Americans even if they are not honorable gentlemen. The late war blew their steam off in no wise. Their hearts were not in it after the first pumped-up and artificially induced hysteria evaporated. Germany had invaded Belgium? Well, Belgium was as remote and unfamiliar a land as Timbuctoo, so what of it? Germany had sunk the *Lusitania?* Well, the *Lusitania,* after all, was an English ship: that, in these grown-up boys' minds was a more important fact than that some Americans had lost their lives on it. The Germans were threatening Paris? The boys looked into their history books and found that the French, for all the beautiful gesture of Lafayette, had charged the United States a pretty stiff fee for sending help over in the American Revolutionary War.

And, anyway, these little boys, now grown up, had no fond recollections of Belgian, English and French boys as they had of German boys. The family butcher had been a German and his little son had been the delivery boy who, after the meat in the brown paper had been deposited at the back door, was impressed into service for a game of duck-on-rock in a neighboring alley. The man who ran the corner saloon had been a German who let the little boys crawl under the swinging rattan doors and who shut his eyes when they stole pretzels from the wicker basket at the door-end of the bar. The cook had been a German woman, and the little boys, grown up, still remembered her Christmas cookies. The policeman had been a German—for that was before the Irish got control of the force—and the little boys forgot his having chased them off the streets for playing tag on the car tracks in the memory of the hearty, brotherly handshake he gave them when he came around annually on Christmas morning to collect the usufructs of Christian amity for having kept burglars away on the preceding 364 nights. The baker had been a German and, as the little boys recalled, he "wouldn't hurt a flea." The four-piece band that had played such magnificent tunes in front of the house in those years long gone was composed of Germans; Zimmer, the great baseball hero of those days, was a German; the "Lilliputians," who gave the first grand theatre show that these little boys had been allowed to go to, were Germans; Sandow, the strong man and their boyhood god, was a German; the first tune that every one of their piano teachers taught them was *"Du, du, liegst mir im Herzen"*; all the toys that made their youngsterhood happy had been marked "Made in Germany"; the wonderful and envied acrobats at the circus were Germans; and the Grimms, whose fairy tales their mothers had read to them, were Germans. It was pretty hard to hate the Germans, the little boys in khaki and with real guns in place of the old air-rifles found. The Germans had never done anything to them, they considered, and, after the first flare and novelty of adventure wore off, the little boys in khaki and with real guns in place of the old air-rifles began to see things a little differently from Woodrow Wilson, who, after all, they reminded themselves, was a lot more English than nine-tenths of them were.

These boy-men's eyes turn presently to adventure in another direction and, save I am sorely mistaken, that direction is England. For this, I for one, as an American, am sorry. Though I have no English blood in me, I admire England and the English, the land and its people. I have spent parts of many happy years in that tranquil and comfortable and lovely country, and, among my closest and most valued friends, there are many, many Britons. I can, therefore, be of no greater service as an honorable friend than to point out to them, truthfully and without the conventional contemptible American hypocrisy, the way the foolish, unfortunate and tragic wind blows.

§ 2

England and the American Language.—One of the things that impresses itself most forcibly about

88

England in late years is the spread of the so-called American language there and the extent to which it has usurped the English of the English. Ten years back it was often as difficult for the American to understand what an Englishman was driving at as it was for the latter to understand what the American was trying to say. Today, little such trouble exists. With American books flooding the bookstalls, American magazines—sometimes published under other names, *e. g., Nash's*, etc.—on every hand, American plays occupying seventy-five per cent of the English theatres, American movies with their American sub-titles on every other street, Americans figuring prominently in the English horse world and so on, the American language has filtered through British life to a remarkable degree, and it is today a rare Englishman who is not as familiar with the cat's pajamas, banana oil and the condition of one's old man as any native of Eighth avenue.

When George Ade's "The College Widow" was produced in London some years ago, it was a flat failure. The English couldn't make head or tail of its language, even though a glossary was handed out to each member of the audience. Today, "Is Zat So?" which would have been completely unintelligible to an Englishman, whether in the stalls or in the pit, ten years ago, is a huge success. Anita Loos' "Gentlemen Prefer Blondes," which is full of presumably exotic Americanisms, becomes the best selling book in England. Cabell, who writes the English of the English, attracts little notice, where Sinclair Lewis, who is as American in speech as Babe Ruth, is quoted wherever one goes. The Englishman of today knows exactly what the American means when he says elevator instead of lift, when he orders a Hamburger instead of a Salisbury, when he alludes to a sightseer instead of a charabanc, when he shouts Bronx, Manhattan or Alexander, when he orders a derby instead of a bowler or a sailor instead of a boating-straw, when he refers to tin lizzies or speak-easys, when he says "Step on it," "Beat it," "sap," "simp," "eyewash" and even "the bum's rush." American speech, together with its custom, has taken so great a hold on England, indeed, that certain of the old English taboos are no longer operative, as, for example, in the case of such words as "stomach" and "bloody," both of which are now used commonly in polite society. The most generally employed exclamation in England today is "Gosh," borrowed from the American corn-belt. The expression is no longer "top hole" nor "ripping," but "great" or "dandy." As an experiment in London one day not long ago I tried speaking absolutely un-American English of the vintage of some years back to an English friend of mine. He didn't know what I was talking about.

§ 3

The Change in Our Brother.—The constantly increasing, palpable and ominous lack of self-confidence on the part of the Englishman, once the most resolutely self-assured of mortals, is of a high significance in more directions than one. There was a time when the Englishman, criticized by men of other nations, simply paid not the slightest attention to what was being said, and treated his critics to a very elegant species of monocled disdain. In that day, the Englishman, like all men certain of their superiority, with an airy disregard brushed aside criticism of himself and his country as he would have brushed aside a slightly irritating but entirely harmless and ineffectual flea. To-day, however, a change has come over our brother across the sea, as ever a change comes over men when they grow to be less sure of themselves. To-day, the Englishman resents, and bitterly, all criticism of himself and his country from outsiders. The most trivial derogation of his eminence in any one of the world's affairs, from stoking a battle cruiser to confecting a novel, disturbs his peace of mind and arouses his dander. He has become doubtful of himself, of his virtuosity, of the erstwhile impregnability of his position and of the position of his nation. He currently reveals himself, in his advancing sensitiveness and in the thinness of his skin, as one with unmistakable misgivings and forebodings. Every time an Englishman writes a hot letter to the *Times* protesting against something that has been said about England by an American, every time an Englishman irately denounces an American to the ship news reporters for having observed that cricket is less exciting sport than football or that one can get a better shampoo and a glossier shoeshine over here than one can get

in London, the fly that has appeared in the oint-
ment of his national and personal security is readily
to be detected. Men's indignation increases as their
self-trust and self-reliance decrease.

THE MUSE IN OUR MIDST

§ 1

Cabell and Lewis.—Among the gentry currently practising the art of beautiful letters amongst us, just two, the inevitable Dreiser excepted, I allow myself to believe, will be read by our grandchildren. These two are the MM. Cabell and Lewis. And why? Because these two alone have in their work the portents of longevity: the former, a beauty of prose that must outlive its time, and the latter a sound commentary on the civilization of his epoch that must carry into the future years its reflective burden of curiosity and illumination. There are, true enough, a number of other considerable fiction talents gladdening the present-day scene; some of them are talents of undisputed force; but they strike me as being merely of, by and for the moment. There is little in the work they are producing that can withstand the forces of time. The materials they deal with, though often ably handled and not without an immediate eloquence, are evanescent for all their apparent feeling of truth and humanity. The stories they tell are often moving, but thousands of stories that have been equally moving in years that are gone have long since passed from the attention and even the memory of living readers. Mere truth, mere artistry, mere conviction do not always parade down the decades. It takes something more than these. Beauty, sheer beauty and nothing more, lives on long after impressive narratives less blessed have disappeared from the public shelves. A study of the times and the manners of the times and the thought of the times, set forth in terms of an outstanding and recognizable institution or character, outlives ten thousand books that merely tell an insignificant story with brilliance.

§ 2

The Message of Art.—As ridiculous as the theory that great art exercises an ennobling influence upon man and inculcates in him a prompt and overwhelming passion for close psychic association with God, the angels and the League for the Enforcement of Prohibition, is the sister theory that great art must inevitably carry a message to man. Great art, in point of fact, carries no such thing; rather is it great art for the directly opposite reason. It carries with it, true enough, the message of its own technical beauty, but to call that a message, in the way the word is generally used, is like saying that sauerkraut carries with it its own taste and katharsis. Everything has its message, if one wishes to put a fine point upon mundane phenomena and if one has a mind to make the language conceal the nonsense of one's reasoning; but art, precisely speaking, has no other actual message than its internal dignity and splendor. What, conceivably, is the nature of the "message" of "Huckleberry Finn," of the "Iliad," of Michelangelo's sculpture, of a Brahms trio, of Raphael's portrait of himself, or of the Grand Central Station? The message in each of these cases is simply, and nothing more, than this: that a great artist has achieved perfect form in his own particular domain of art. That is the only message that real art carries. The messages that certain critics speak of—these critics who conceive of art as a branch of the Western Union—are reserved for imitations of authentic art. Maeterlinck's "Blue Bird," Gounod's "Nazareth" and Longfellow's "Hiawatha" have messages and duly convey them to the boobs, but Shakespeare's "Twelfth Night," a Beethoven fantasia and Chaucer's "The Assembly of Fowls" have no more of a message than so many brilliant stars in the heavens. There are certain exceptions, of course, as there are always exceptions. But, taking great art on the whole, we find it to be as devoid of evangelism as a perfect Spring day, a perfect flower, or any other such analogous masterpiece of God's making.

§ 3

The Decline of the Short Story.—That the American novel has advanced out of all proportion to the American short story in the last fifteen years is pretty well agreed. Just why the shorter form of fiction has been left far behind in the matter of relative quality has been puzzling the diagnosticians. Many reasons have been offered, some of them convincing. But one reason, more convincing than the rest, I believe, has been overlooked. And that reason is to be found in the illustrated magazines.

It is of course, a platitude that fiction is critically estimable in the degree that it creates authentic character. While our better novelists have duly concerned themselves with this requisite of their art, our short story writers have not. Few novelists worth considering look to the magazines for revenue from the sale of their work. The magazines, illustrated or not, use very few novels or serial stories. For one novel, they use seventy-five or a hundred short stories. The magazines are thus a direct market, and a very good one, for the short story writers, who rely almost entirely upon the proceeds therefrom for their livelihood. There is little money in most books made up of short stories, whereas there is considerable in novels. The novelist may thus trust to his book sales for his income, but the short story writer may not. Not being able to, the latter must write with the magazines in mind rather than the book publisher, and he must turn out a great deal more work. But this is not the point. The point, rather, is that, having to turn out a relatively large number of short stories to make a living, he soon grows careless in the fabrication of characters that shall be vivid to the reader and lazily leaves the job to the magazine illustrators. He allows the pictures to do what he doesn't do. He relies upon the illustrations to give his readers an idea of his characters and confines himself more and more to plot, action and the general externals of fiction. He knows from experience that the editors of the illustrated magazines, which are the big-paying ones, do not care for character analysis, "descriptions," etc., that they rely, instead, upon lithographs quickly to suggest such things to the impatient reader, and gradually he falls into the habit of omitting them. Many promising short story writers have thus gone down the chute. It would be easy, were one given to impoliteness, to name names. It is not, as is sometimes argued, that these writers have been ruined by writing short stories to order—as a matter of fact, short stories are seldom written to order, since editors are not such fools as to buy fiction in advance of reading it; it is simply that the writers have ruined themselves by writing toward magazine illustrations instead of away from them. With a single exception, there is not a first-rate writer of short stories in America today whose work has appeared regularly in the illustrated periodicals. I believe that there is considerable significance in the fact.

§ 4

Ayer's Almanac.—This is the seventy-fourth anniversary of the American comedic menopause known as *Ayer's Almanac,* founded by Dr. James C. Ayer, of Lowell, Mass., and for seventy-four consecutive years the butt of all Americans of a facetious turn of mind. Far above the name of Joe Miller, far above that of the Benevolent Protective Order of Elks, far above even that of the gas-house, has its name been invoked to stigmatize and dismay the unhappy humorous writer, playwright, stage clown and after-dinner orator. It has been the synonym *summa cum* for sour jokes, the cuspidor of a hundred thousand derisions. Yet it is doubtful if even one of the persons who has used its name in vain has ever actually taken a look at it. And, in this respect, I have the honor to offer myself as Exhibit A. For years I have slung the custard of my irony at it in company with everyone else, yet only today did it occur to me that it mightn't be a bad idea to glance at the thing and see what it was like.

The humor of *Ayer's Almanac,* estimating it from the copy at hand, is, contrary to the general impression, not such dismal stuff after all. Not rib-busting, perhaps, but comedy of a very fair sort, quite as serviceable as any you will find in the humorous weeklies or in the musical comedies and revues. For example:

Teacher: Do you understand the difference between liking and loving?

Willie: Yes, ma'am; I like my father and mother, but I love pie.

Again:

Passenger *(to chauffeur)*: Hey! you've run over a man. Aren't you going to stop?

Chauffeur: Naw! I can read all about it in the papers.

Still again—to return to little Wilhelm and Teacher:

Teacher: Willie, give me three proofs that the world is actually round.

Willie: Yes'm. The book says so, you say so, and ma says so.

And still again:

Hay and Feed Dealer: you owe me $3 for oats, Mose, and if you don't pay me I'll have to take your horse.

Uncle Mose: All right, Mista Guggenheimer, an' Ah'll pay you de balance o' de $3 just as soon as Ah kin.

Here, true enough, is not precisely the species of jocosity to floor one, yet is it any worse than that which our highly paid magazine and stage comedians get by with?

In *Ayer's* I find this:

Doctor (*to Atchison dinge*): What did your father die of?
Dinge: Ah don't know, boss, but it wasn't nothin' serious.

In the latest piece of literature by the man who is regarded by Americans as their leading humorist and whose work is reviewed at length in the literary weeklies, I find this:

Love makes the world go round because every lover is a crank.

And this:

Why does a dressmaker never lose her hooks?
Because, my dear, she has an eye to each of them.

§ 5

The Ladies and the Muse.—Discussing the subject recently with a number of the more prominent lecture bureaux managers, I discover that my old contention that women are interested in the arts chiefly in proportion to the physical pulchritude of their exponents finds an increasingly disconcerting substantiation. These lecture managers tell me that the majority of women's clubs throughout the country have during the last year thrown off their former false-faces in very large part and have at last honestly come forth and affirmed, albeit occasionally indirectly, that they want no more bald, knock-kneed, bow-legged, undersized or ancient male spectacles for their platforms and that, if they are to be elevated and to pay for that elevation, they want the elevating to be done by men whom they can look at without disappointment and pain, and perhaps even with hope. The statistics of the lecture bureaux show conclusively that personable performers bring out the girls in large numbers, whereas less sightly fellows play to very poor houses indeed. In Chicago, for example, a lecturer on literature with the face and shape of a movie actor not long ago so crowded a certain women's club that two hundred extra chairs had to be rented at the last moment from a near-by undertaking parlor, where another, himself a figure of high importance in the art of which he spoke, but unfortunately of a close personal resemblance to a beer-keg, drew exactly ten women out of the club's roster of one hundred and seventy-two.

The situation has grown alarming so far as the lecture bureaux gentlemen are concerned, and they frankly admit it. Of the English and American lecturers on literature, drama and the other arts whose names appear on their books, not more than two out of fifty are what may be termed pretty fellows. The others, estimable though they be, could hardly be described even as passable. For all their intelligence and talent, their hair is thin on top, or their middles are too greatly remindful of misplaced bustles, or their clothes are of the walk-up variety, or their chins are plural, or their teeth are bad. Up to a comparatively short time ago, these hapless fellows were still able to discharge their funds of æsthetic wisdom to a substantial profit and were able to hold the girls in their seats while they discoursed learnedly on Romain Rolland, Hardy, Einstein, the Irish Movement and topics of a kidney. But their day is apparently done. The girls are through with them. What the girls want is not a lecture on Hardy by a man four feet tall with large ears, but one on A. A. Milne or Compton Mackenzie—or, for that matter, on Felix the Cat or ping-pong—by one with soft eyes, black, curly hair and a build like a piano-mover. What they want is not the lecture, but the lecturer.

This, surely, is not news; it is the recent statistics on the subject that give the old news a measure of piquancy. Art, so far as the women's clubs go, is simply a refuge from husbands. Its beauty—or, at least, the small measure of its beauty that they are able to understand and appreciate—makes up to them some of the beauty in which their home and daily lives are lacking. But, since they are usually incapable of deriving a sufficient degree of that beauty from the particular art itself, they are inevitably driven to the device of extracting it from the man who is acting as the interpreter of the art. They allow their repining gaze to rest admiringly and mayhap longingly upon the lovely gent on the platform and in their dreams they achieve a touch of vicarious gratification. This latter they cannot get from a fellow physically unfavored by God, however great an artist he may be; they can get it only from one, whatever his incapacity in his profession, who looks nothing like their husbands and whose voice, while it is ostensibly occupying itself with the æsthetic doctrines of Copenhagen cubist painters or Czechoslovakian *vers-librists*, has the undertones of an Anatol or a Casanova. And thus it is that the lecture managers, to ward off starvation, have of necessity been driven to the expedient of planning a doubly increased fee next season for lecturers who look more like potential lovers than like talented painters, novelists, dramatists and poets.

§ 6

Gaul and Anglo-Saxon.—The Englishman and American write of women as men know them; the

Frenchman writes of women as women know them.

§ 7

The Conversation of Artists.—The reason for the dullness of the conversation of artists, at least as it rebounds from the tympani of non-artists, is easily arrived at. The fundamentals and even the curlicues of any art, from music to architecture and from literature to sculpture, are completely Greek to the non-artist, as they are, indeed, to many hypothetical artists, and—even were they not —contain in them no more of the juices and essences of entertaining discourse than the pterygoid fossa or the theological predilections of Hollywood. The conversation of the non-artist, on the other hand, even when it is not interesting, is at least intelligible to other non-artists as to artists themselves. It is impossible to imagine an engaging stock-broker or Pullman porter being held at rapt attention by the locution of a Beethoven, but it is surely very easy to imagine a Beethoven being deeply interested in the palaver of a stockbroker or Pullman porter. It is equally difficult to imagine a Babbitt understanding what a poet means when

he speaks of the dactylic hexameter or holo-
spondaic verse, but it takes no overly gifted fancy
to imagine a poet understanding perfectly, and
even being interested in, the details of the fold-
ing-bed business, the manufacture of pies, and
holeproof socks.

§ 8

The Literature of the Negro.—The literature of the
Negro pours from the presses as never before in
publishing history. A week does not pass that
Negro poems, songs, autobiographies, novels and
what not, do not jostle for favor on the book stalls
with the masterpieces of Blasco Ibañez, the Rev.
Thomas Dixon and other such representatives of
the white, or superior, race. Many of these Negro
opera are highly commendable; many throw an
illuminating light upon the hopes, dreams, achieve-
ments, character and psyche of our black fellow
citizens. But, of them all, there is one, published
some months ago and designed for the Negro trade
alone, that has thus far been reviewed in not a
single Caucasian publication and that is yet perhaps the most remarkable of the lot in showing the

trend of the Negro mind as it operates today in certain eminent colorado maduro circles. I allude to "The Black Man, the Father of Civilization," by James Morris Webb, A.M., issued by the Royal Messenger Press of Chicago, Ill.

Dr. Webb, it appears, has no misgivings as to the future of his race. He bases his claims on its past performances, some of which will come in the way of news to his white readers. For example, he states: "The black colonial troops and other black subjects of the British and French government, also the American black Yanks, made it possible for the Allied nations to drive a peace victory over Germany and her allies. The black man was the backbone of it all, just as much so as he was the backbone of the Union army which made it possible for General Grant to receive General Lee's sword as a token of surrender." But this is not all. "When the Kaiser's army tried to capture Paris twice and failed," continues Dr. Webb, "no doubt General Hindenburg reported to the Kaiser that the Colonial and other black troops from Africa were the backbone of the French and British armies and that it was impossible to get into Paris.

Again, no doubt, the Kaiser said, 'Well, Hindenburg, make a stand-pat Hindenburg line.' So this was done. But when the Kaiser had been told that a black American Yank had captured ten German soldiers by himself and other black Yanks were doing similar heroic acts, it became too much for the Kaiser to stand and hence the Hindenburg line began to weaken. Especially when Sergeant William Butler, the black Yank of New York, rescued his white lieutenant and a number of privates from the German side, the Kaiser ordered his army to gradually give the Hindenburg line up and finally the Kaiser gave up the sponge to the Allies."

From this, the eminent Doctor proceeds to the theory that the fifth universal kingdom of earth, foretold by "the black prophet, Daniel," will be ruled by a black man with woolly hair. "Yes," says Dr. Webb, "his hair will be like pure wool, and the sheep and the Negro have the only pure wool, as see Daniel, VII, 9." But wait! "To prove that this King will be a black man (Negro or colored), Jacob on his dying bed prophesied that He would be an offspring of his son Judah (Genesis, XLIX, 10). This Judah married two Hamite (black, colored or Negro) women. . . . The blood still stands, for if the blood of the Negro becomes fused in a family by marriage or in any other way, the offspring are Negroes. The Virgin Mary, the mother of Jesus, was born out of the tribe of Judah, a black tribe, so therefore Jesus, the Son of God, could not escape the blood of the Negro. After Jesus was born, a decree went forth from Herod to slay Him. God viewed all Europe and Asia to find a place of rescue, but sad to say none was found. But, fortunately, when God looked over Africa, the black belt, He located a spot on the River Nile, the River Nile where every spoke of the wheel of civilization was borne by black men and women, and He immediately sent an angel to warn Joseph in a dream to accompany Mary and the young child to Egypt. If Jesus had been an Anglo-Saxon child, it seems natural that God would have had him rescued by the Anglo-Saxon race, but as Jesus was related to the black race by blood, it was God's own business to have the Babe of Bethlehem rescued and rocked in the black man's cradle."

The author of this unusual tome, so much having been established by him, next takes up, in order, proofs (1) that it was the white man, not the Negro, who was the deviser of poisonous alcoholic tipples; (2) that the Negro "has ranked as high in society as it was possible for man to go"; (3) that "no law of man will ever keep the white and black races from amalgamating"; (4) that Abraham, the father of the Jews, married a Negress; (5) that Moses married several Negresses; (6) that there are at present 12,000,000 people in the United States who, though neither black nor white, are called Negroes—the responsible persons, the author observes ironically, being "our white brethren who took charge of us against our will and started out to teach us civilization and religion when we were heathens"; (7) that "two of the Twelve Apostles were Negroes, to wit, Barnabas and Simon (see Acts XIII, I)"; (8) that Judah, of whom Christ was to come, married descendants of Canaan, son of Ham, who was the father of all Ethiopians; (9) that "Solomon, the great, wise son of David, was a Negro (see the Songs of Solomon, 1, 5 and 6)"; (10) that "Solomon's most royal guest after the dedication of the temple was a Negro woman, the Queen of Sheba (see I Kings, X, 1)"; (11) that "the royal Jew during Solomon's time was black and the common Jew white"; and (12) that "Bathsheba, before becoming David's wife, had been the wife of a Negro."

Now will the membership committee of the Klan hang its head in shame?

§ 9

50–50.—Nothing is so ruinous to an artist as a love of money. Nothing is so ruinous to a business man as a love of art.

§ 10

The Overwhelming Genius of Literary America.— 1. "Romancer, soldier, poet, gallant sportsman, great artist and great man, a Donn Byrne is born to bless this drab world of ours with his bold, colorful, high-hearted stories once in a hundred years. A nobler Byron, a more musical Dumas, a more vital Meredith, a swifter moving Scott—here he

is, Donn Byrne! No man can tell a story like him."
—*The Century Magazine*.

2. "One must go back to Dickens to find anything that so combines pathos and humor as Barry Benefield's 'The Chicken-Wagon Family.' "—*The Bookman*.

3. "Henry Sydnor Harrison is a combination of Swift and Thackeray."—Nashville *Banner*.

4. "William McFee puts Waldo Frank's new book, 'Virgin Spain,' by the side of Keyserling, Doughty and Emerson."—New York *World*.

5. "T. S. Stribling is an artist equal to Zola."—Toledo, O., *Blade*.

6. "Mary Roberts Rinehart is a story-teller superior to Dumas and Fielding."—Los Angeles *Daily News*.

7. "Thornton Niven Wilder, author of 'The Cabala,' who is only twenty-nine, comes before the world with a style distinguished by maturity and by an exquisite sense of tonal values, subdued to a perfect and supple instrument of literary expression. He uses words with the professional sense of color and numerical weight of a gambler dealing a faro bank. His style bears comparison with

Pater. . . . It suggests one of those wonderful clocks made by medieval craftsmen which, when other timepieces merely strike twelve, keep track of sidereal and ecclesiastical time and mark the phases of the moon with meticulous accuracy . . ."—New York *Times Book Review*.

8. "In H. C. Witwer, America has a humorous writer without an equal."—Roanoke, Va., *Times*.

9. "No writer, not even the mighty Kipling, can paint a word picture with half the warmth and color of Achmed Abdullah. In this respect he stands unequaled by any author in the history of English literature."—Minneapolis *Star*.

10. "Arthur J. Rees has the valued gift possessed by Stevenson and Poe."—New York *Herald-Tribune Books*.

11. " . . . Paul Green is doing for America what Synge has already done for Ireland."—*Ditto*.

12. "Nowhere on Anita Loos' countenance can there be found the faintest trace of that super-sophisticated wisdom and cynical knowledge of life and men and women that would have drawn the respect of Rabelais and the envy of Voltaire." —*The Theatre Magazine*.

13. "Only a Dumas could conceive fiction that equaled 'The Rosalie Evans Letters.'"—Gertrude Atherton in the *International Book Review*.

14. "Edward Lautenbach has the art of Stevenson and Poe looking pale blue. Sentences from him are evolved in the rhythm of the stars, borne earthward on the wings of angels."—New Haven, Conn., *Union*.

§ 11

Woman as Artist.—One of the favorite perplexities of the student of æsthetics concerns the seeming paradox that woman, the more emotional of the sexes, occupies, in the practice of the arts, a position of so great inferiority to relatively unemotional and rational man. Since art, the student argues, is the retailing of emotion in terms of beauty, why should not woman, the emotional creature, surpass or at least equal man, the unemotional creature? If it were true that the definition of art were precisely that which the student postures, that is, if art reposed chiefly in emotion, one might lift an eyebrow with him. But the fact is that the accepted definition is faulty to a considerable degree. Art is itself not emotion. Art simply conveys to another an emotion which the artist himself has carefully and painstakingly filtered through a meditative and critical mind. Woman lacks this quality of mind and as a result we have her inability to convey emotion with the force, the beauty and the conviction of man.

The woman in the arts, with very few exceptions, has sought to inspire emotion in terms of emotion, which is very much like trying to inspire a warmth of the heart by burning a person's house down upon him. If art consisted solely in the emotionalization of the beholder, woman would have occupied many more niches in its high temple. But art consists rather in an enkindling of the heart and fancy through the mind. The greatest art appeals first to the mind, and then to the heart. That is why culture, experience and a critical equipment are necessary to a proper understanding and appreciation of great art, and why, on the other hand, those without these gifts are unable to understand and appreciate it. To anyone, even to the humblest of God's blockheads, simple emotion is intelligible, and easy to assimilate, and easier still to react to. But a reaction to an emotion created out of an artist's profound thought is far beyond the reach of such a one's sensibilities. The emotional blockhead can readily comprehend and react to such performances as George Sand's "Consuelo," Rosa Bonheur's "The Horse Fair," Thela Badarczevska's "La Prière d'une Vierge" or the Black Patti, but it takes a sophisticated and intelligent emotionalism to comprehend and properly to react to Flaubert's "Sentimental Education," Rubens' "Fall of the Damned," a Bach fugue or Feodor Chaliapin.

§ 12

The Value of Censorship.—There is at least one point in connection with literary and dramatic censorship that most of its foes overlook and that point is that it very directly operates to improve craftsmanship in the field of lovely letters. Finding that their wares, because of the literality of their expression, fall under the censors' ban, authors who otherwise might rest content lazily to exploit the relatively simple pronouncements of realism are driven to the more intricate and trying art of literary suggestion, implication and inference. An imagination is now called upon that was previously called upon but feebly. The author is put to it to defeat censorship with the devious complexities of the literary art, the subtle shadings, the fine circumlocutions, all the shrewd and masterly jugglings of the English language. It is and it will ever be thus that a Cabell, who knows how to write, will always beat the censors after the first skirmish, where a lesser skill at English composition will be pounced upon and devoured.

ASPECTS OF THE CONTEMPORARY SCENE

§ 1

The Crime Wave.—That the recent tremendous spread of crime in the United States is due to any one or all of the reasons assigned, I seriously doubt. The responsibility has been placed upon everything from the late war to the modern novel, from Bolshevism to bad booze, and from insufficient police protection to the automobile and the easy means of escape provided by the latter. That these have been the mainspring of the crime wave does not convince me. Unless I am uncommonly mistaken, the responsibility lies in a different quarter and that is the enormous increase in the number of shady, but shrewd and competent, shyster lawyers who have sprung up like mushrooms all over the country. These fellows, out for notoriety and money and willing to do anything to get them, have opened offices in almost every other block of every American town of any size. And their trade consists in large part of taking on as clients gentlemen who have illegally gotten away with swag of one kind or another and in getting as much of it as possible for themselves. They have nothing to lose and everything to gain. If they can prove the innocence of their clients or even merely that their clients no longer have the swag in their possession (whatever may happen to the clients after that), they are down in their luck if at least half of the cabbaged boodle doesn't find its way into their pockets. If, on the other hand, their clients go to the hoosegow, they are out only a little gab and time.

The crooks have been trained to know these shysters and to put confidence in them. And that confidence has been well repaid. Twenty years ago, a criminal had difficulty in getting a lawyer to handle his case for him. Today, a dozen are waiting for him when the patrol-wagon backs up to the police station. These shysters, as I have said, are not merely charlatans; many of them have legal minds devious, sharp and immensely cunning. Glance at the newspapers any day and you will read a sufficiently illuminating record of their successes. Against the overcrowded and tired court mind, a mind that has utterly no time to do justice to the prosecution, their own alert mind has a comparatively easy job. Only in the case of murder do they experience any difficulty and even here the statistics show a remarkable record of good fortune for them.

This new genus shyster is a fellow far superior in trickery to his brother of the past. He has made a study of it and has mastered it. The old shyster was simply a snide lawyer with a couple of political friends upon whom he had something, who were hence in his power and whom he could use to his client's advantage, plus a shabby Prince Albert and a loud mouth; but the shyster of today is no such low fowl. He knows criminal law inside and out, chiefly inside, and he is privy to the means as how best to jockey it in his client's favor. The criminal classes read that he has succeeded in getting Abe Flopbaum off easily by proving that Abe was dropped on the head when three years old and was therefore not in his right senses when he forged the check for $30,000, that he has managed to

122

free Luigi the Wop by proving that the mulatto whose body was found in the sewer was the one actually responsible for the seduction of the Swedish servant girl, and that he got Aloysius Mulcahey, Jr., out of Sing Sing by showing that one of the jurors who convicted him was a Ku Kluxer, and they thereupon hitch up their trousers, get out the old family six-shooter and go out and hold up another Columbus avenue jeweler and make off with another quart of diamonds.

In any city where there are as many lawyers as policemen, crime is in high feather. The towns that have few lawyers in them are invariably found to be happy, peaceful and law-abiding communities.

§ 2

The Klan and the Press.—Outside of the South, it is probably a fair estimate to say that fully three-quarters of the more important newspapers of the Republic have been and are, either openly or in spirit, against the Grand and Exalted Order of Ku Kluxers These papers have for three years now opposed the Klan in their news and editorial

123

columns. They have often colored the news deliberately to the Klan's disadvantage and their editorials have denounced the organization as being anti-American, corrupt, a danger to the Union, an inciter of race prejudice, a violator of the Constitution and a hundred other such pestiferous cocci. And yet, today, the Klan still flourishes. The journalistic bird-shot has rolled off its back like water off a duck's. Why?

Whenever the matter has been discussed, the reasons commonly assigned have had to do with the decline of journalistic influence in America, yet it seems to me that only a very unobservant person can bring himself to believe that this influence is not every bit as strong today as it ever has been. The reason must be looked for in another quarter, and that quarter, I believe, is not in the newspaper columns but in the Klan itself. Above everything else, above each and all of its open pretensions, above even its political and sectarian cut, the Klan is a club formed by men of common likes and dislikes and of mutual tastes, and a newspaper can no more break up such a fellowship by calling it names and arousing those on the outside than it can bring the Union League Club to serve six oysters on a plate instead of five. Newspaper readers, even where they are most strongly opposed to the conduct and actions of the Klan, feel instinctively that, above its public manifestations, it is, in a manner of speaking, a private organization, like the Elks, the Knights of Pythias or the Beethoven Association, and as such entitled to its place in the community life. All the jokes of the last twenty years haven't disbanded the Elks; all the jazz of the next twenty will not disband the Beethoven Association; all the abuse of the newspapers cannot succeed in disrupting the Klan. The average American may have many faults, but one of them is not a nosey viciousness when it comes to his fellow American's social federations. And the Klan is, in strict analysis, such a social federation before it is anything else. Had it had the sagacity to choose a more fortunate name for itself, a name in the public eye less symbolic of masked banditry, some such name, let us say, as the Society for American Peace or the Sons of the Republic, no one would ever have heard so much as a peep against it.

§ 3

Fortune-Tellers.—In the crusade of the ordained constabulary against clairvoyants, crystal-gazers, fortune-tellers, palmists and other such professors of the joys and sorrows of tomorrow, one detects the usual American official device of making a great show by hitting such members of the community as have no power to strike back. The authorities are simply up to their now venerable trick of blinking conveniently when the bloodhounds go by and of displaying their strength against the helpless mutts. If there were so many as two millionaires or two men with political power who were to don black velvet peignoirs, smell up their back parlors with corner drugstore incense and begin to predict magnificent amours to old girls with double chins, the authorities would indulge in a second thought before proceeding against the professional seers either in part or as a whole. But as the prognosticating profession is made up entirely of nothing more impressive and dismaying than ex-dentists, gynecologists who have lost their licenses, Armenian rug dealers who have exhausted their easy pickings and Jewish drummers who have grown long moustaches and changed their names to Abdul, Yasim and Hamid, the gendarmerie has nothing to hold it back and accordingly lets moral nature take its course.

Yet what is the specific charge against these soothsayers? The charge against them is that they swindle the public by professing to do something that is not within their power. They take money on the theory that they are able to foretell events, on the presumption that they are privy to the secrets of the future, on the assurance that they can indicate cures, alleviate ills and suggest the means of future well-being. Well, so do the chiropractors and osteopaths; so do the gentlemen of the clergy; so do the stock and bond dealers of Wall Street; so do the Florida realtors; so do the advertisers who guarantee that they can grow hair on bald heads, teach the piano by mail in thirty days, and make a brilliant conversationalist and great social favorite out of a mill-hand. These persons, however, unlike the fortune-tellers, have, the most of them, organizations of their own kind to protect them or influence enough in one direction or another to keep the civic uhlans from making raids upon them. Yet they are, in their several ways, equally dubious. If a fortune-teller predicts that a client will make a pot of money if he invests his hard-earned savings in this or that oil stock, the stock-broker does the same thing; and one's guess is as good as the other's. If a fortune-teller promises future happiness or future woe, so does a clergy-man. And if a fortune-teller suggests to his client that a magnetized horseshoe carried in the rear pants pocket will cure his long-standing thrombolymphangitis, a chiropractor tells his that a manipulation of one of his ribs will cure his long-standing gout, gall-stones, dandruff, stammering and loss of hearing.

If the police run the fortune-tellers out of town and permit the rev. clergy to remain, where the justice? If it is against the law and public welfare to put on a black bath-robe embroidered with silver stars, smell up the place with punk sticks and tell a fat woman that she is going to meet a handsome dark man sometime in the near future, why should it be permissible to put on a black frock coat with one's collar turned around, smell up the place with punk sticks and tell the same fat woman that she is going to meet Jesus sometime in the perhaps more distant future? That the fat woman may, and, indeed, sometimes actually does, meet her brunet desideratum, the police know, or can easily verify the one way or the other—and act accordingly. But is there a single policeman, however gifted, who can say for a certainty that she will meet the Lord God Almighty Himself when she shuffles off? Although I have faith in the efficiency of the police force, I doubt it. If, accordingly, it is just to give the bum's rush to a man who looks into a glass paper-weight and gratifyingly predicts that General Motors will go up, why shouldn't it be equally just to give the bum's rush to one who looks into a black-bound book and gratifyingly predicts that general humanity will do the same thing?

§ 4

System.—I recently had occasion to do some business with a shop whose proprietors and managers boast that it is the most perfectly systematized establishment of its kind in New York. These gentlemen have spent three years, they say, in working

out every last detail of their business machine so
that it will give every last drop of service to themselves and to their customers. Time clocks, check-
ing devices, filing cabinets and mechanical aids of
every sort give the place the look of a suave boiler-
works; the over-clerks, under-clerks and mid-level
clerks have been trained with the precision of German lieutenants; the cab-starter wears as many
medals as General Foch. Thousands upon thousands of dollars, in short, have been spent to make
the store click like an automatic pistol. "All this,"
run the firm's advertisements, "promises those who
deal with us the ultimate in satisfaction." The
other day, as I say, I made a minor business transaction with the firm. It would take ten days, the
person in charge of the department assured me,
to fill my order. I needed what I needed in less
time, but I understood, in turn, the shop's need for
more time, so assented. At the expiration of the
ten days, I called up the store and asked if my
order was ready. I was assured that, true to the
promise given me, it was. I asked that it be sent
to me that day without fail, as I had immediate
need of it. But, I was told, the delivery boys had

already left; it was then four o'clock in the afternoon; and my order therefore couldn't be delivered until the following morning. I requested that the shop have a boy bring the order around to me; it would take only a few minutes, as I lived not three blocks away. That could not be done, I was told, as the organization had no provision for such deliveries; all deliveries had to be made according to the set and systematized schedule. I went to the shop, got my order, and that is the last that that particular perfectly systematized establishment will ever see of me.

This is the sixth time in the last two years that such admirable systematization in six different establishments has lost a hitherto steady customer in me. The trouble with these highly perfected business organizations is a simple one. They work as perfectly as so many machines and, like machines, they lack all personal sense and discrimination. Their managers are tickled to death by the accuracy of service, as it is reported to them on the daily charts, but these managers never know how this very accuracy has alienated customers in one way or another, for the reason that a disgruntled customer usually shuts up and takes his patronage somewhere else. The theory that the way to please a customer is to lay in a patent bundle-wrapper that will tie up his purchase in two minutes, to train the idiot clerk to discourse with him on the state of his health and the British foreign policy while he is waiting and then to have him politely bowed out by a floorwalker with a gardenia in his buttonhole is not quite so sound as the system professors believe. The way to please a customer is not to do everything that he expects the shop to do—the customer takes that as a matter of course; the way to please him is to do various small things that he doesn't expect it to do. But these small things the perfectly systematized shops never take into consideration. And, as a result, they lose customers every day to the little unsystematized concerns who kick the system professors, salesmen of triplicate checking-books, installers of self-opening show-cases, inventors of automatic goods-packers and other such up-to-the-minute nuisances out into the street and install in the stead of them a little old-fashioned trading common sense and a little old-fashioned understanding of human nature. The simple old-time little cigar stores presided over by the affable Gustav Schultzes kept their customers until they died or were sent to jail. The systematized modern cigar stores, with their interiors equipped with every device known to Efficiency, save only the forgotten one of the personal equation, lose theirs weekly. And it is the same with every other kind of shop.

§ 5

Yet Again.—There is no man engaged in business of any kind above street-cleaning who is not made steadily conscious of the inordinate and senseless mass of rigmarole that clutters it up and makes its practice unnecessarily irksome. The simplest business transaction in America today is enveloped in such a mantle of imbecile shenanigan that only a man of the stoutest nerves can go through it without feeling like throwing the office furniture out of the window, hitting his vis-à-vis over the head with the *crachoir* and hopping the first freight to Newfoundland. Conferences utterly without any intelligible purpose, shyster lawyers, system experts, bookkeepers, statisticians, push buttons, profes-

133

sional Cagliostros, typewritten statements that no one can understand, legal documents, two-hour luncheons, long-distance and short-distance telephonings, professors of various occult trade arts— business is presently so full of such time and money wasters that Job himself, were he to sit in an American office for so much as half an hour, would have to get himself completely drunk to be able to stand it.

All this useless to-do, when nine-tenths of the business thus ridiculously beset by unnecessary and empty flummery might be transacted very simply, as it used to be transacted, is due, I daresay, to the overpowering desire of the average American business man to make himself appear to others— and to himself no less—as an important figure. Such a sublime jackass takes pride in making something that is actually very simple seem extremely difficult. He achieves a fine glow from making a mountain out of a molehill and then going in for a lot of hoopdedoodle with irrelevant but imposing-looking alpenstocks. His day is spent in making the easiest transaction as hard as possible; the selling of a gross of neckties is made to take on the aspect of a sale and purchase of the Standard Oil Company. It isn't that he distrusts persons so much as that he distrusts the opinion they may have of him if he doesn't present himself to them in the light of a captain of industry, a master of finance and a regius professor of all the arts of barter.

Now, the moment the business day is over, our friend promptly goes back to normal. Meet him in the evening and you will generally find him to be as simple and forthright a fellow as he was complex and knotty by day. I therefore propose a solution of the present state of affairs that is driving half the more rational business men of the country crazy. I propose that henceforth all American business offices be shut throughout the daytime and that all business be transacted after dark. The suggestion may at the first superficial glance seem foolish, but, appreciating human nature, I believe that it is an eminently sound one and, more, that it will work.

§ 6

The American Traveler.—With the general indignation of American travelers over the way they are being treated in France, the more reputable and intelligent of stay-at-home Americans have considerable difficulty in sympathizing. These returning Americans are greatly worked up over the current genial custom of the French people which substitutes mudpies and bricks for the old Lafayette handshakes, and blackjacks, catcalls and poisoned coffee for the erstwhile kisses on both cheeks. The French, it appears, are ungrateful for the way in which the Americans won the war for them, for democracy and for God—to the French, an insulting reversal of an otherwise satisfactory climacteric phrase—and for the way in which the Americans thereupon quite naturally sent in bills of account. This sad lack of gratitude, exclaim the wrathful *voyageurs*, is being expressed by the Frogs in such objectionable and literal terms as charging an American two thousand francs to get into a peep-show where a Frenchman has to pay only twenty, calling him a *cochon* when he asks for corned beef and cabbage instead of filet de bœuf Renaissance, and hitting him with a cobblestone when, due to the poor quality of French chewing tobacco, he is caused to spit on the tomb of Napoleon.

That the French are not treating American visitors with the same politeness they exhibited toward them before the bills began coming in is certain. But I permit myself an equally certain doubt that they would treat these visitors otherwise even had the Americans helped them quietly in the late unpleasantness, not seduced half of their most personable peasant girls and not subsequently commemorated their nobility of act by presenting the French with statues showing an American doughboy holding hands with Joan of Arc and with bills for several billions of dollars. The war and its incidental concerns have, I believe, very little to do with the French antipathy toward the Americans who spend their holidays in that country. It is, in point of fact, all that the better class of Americans can do to restrain themselves from treating such Americans as go to France in exactly the same way that the French treat them. If Frenchmen came over here in the spirit that Americans go to their country and conducted themselves as Americans do in Paris, the New York streets would be strewn with French whiskers and the electric light posts along Broadway and Fifth Avenue would be spattered with French blood. I have yet to hear of a decent, dignified American being hit over the head in France with a bottle of St. Julien or of one being followed on the boulevards by a crowd of Frenchmen armed with pie à la mode. Whenever you hear of an American who has been booed out of a French restaurant, or had his ear bitten off at the Bal Bullier, or been chased ten blocks by a yelling mob, you may rest assured that the American in question, war or no war, loan or no loan, has done something to merit it. There is no record yet of Frenchmen having pulled the undershirts off Myron T. Herrick, Theodore Dreiser, Jascha Heifetz or Dr. George W. Crile. The records, on the other hand, are full of busted straw hats owned by Americans who have danced the Charleston on Balzac's grave in Père Lachaise, who have sung "Hail, Hail, The Gang's All Here" in the Madeleine, and who have tried to get a Bronx cocktail at the Bibliothèque National. So much is so much. Those who believe that the French are

138

putting bichloride of mercury in Americans' drinks because Coolidge's bills for arms and ammunition service is so big that the French find difficulty in paying it may be reminded that Beaumarchais' bill for the same kind of service in the Revolutionary War was so big that the Americans found equal difficulty in paying it—and that, nevertheless, any decent and dignified French traveler is still perfectly safe and comfortable in the United States.

§ 7

The Frenchman and the Bath.—One of the immemorial pieces of jocosity among Americans, its foundation rooted more or less in fact, concerns the anatomical hydrophobia of the French. That the Frenchman substitutes a pinch of talcum for the tub and that the Saturday night bath joke has no point in France save one specify, in addition, the month and year, have been among the standard articles in the credo of the western countries for a century or more. Recent developments, however, indicate that a change is dawning and that it will not be many years before the bathtub is at least as familiar to Frenchmen as it is to West Virginians.

Mr. George Cecil, a special investigator employed by the *American Druggist*, recently made a tour of France to ascertain, through soap sales, just how far the grievous situation had turned for the better. He discovered that the sale of soap among Frenchmen showed a remarkable increase since the conclusion of the late war. But, though his report was highly interesting in a statistical direction, one or two points that have an illuminating bearing upon the situation appear to have eluded him.

Although the fact has not thus far been made public, I am reliably informed that the popularization of soap among the French has been due in no small measure to the activity and ingenuity of the nation's Ministry of Fine Arts. Mr. Cecil, in his report, has duly noted the new ways in which soap in France is put up, and, also, the new names and fragrances that have been imparted to it, but he has missed drawing the important conclusion between cause and effect. For many, many years, the cheaper grades of soap made in France and designed for home consumption—as opposed to the fancier and tonier soaps designed for export— were unattractively packed, unattractively labeled and but mildly scented. There was nothing about them, in a word, to inflame the fancy of the Frenchman and persuade him to them. The export soaps with their gaudier aspects were too expensive for him and, besides, were seldom displayed in the French shops. What he saw therein, if he so much as looked at them, were soaps so unalluring and homely that they revolted him. This fact the Ministry of Fine Arts took cognizance of a few years ago, and promptly took steps to correct. True enough, the department went at the business of improving the national condition in an indirect and *sotto voce* manner, but at it it went none the less. The first move it made was to get the manufacturers of soap for the home trade to abandon the plain and unattractive wrappers of the past and to hire skilful color artists to design wrappers and cartons that would engage and enchant the impressionable French eye. In a short time, accordingly, no less than sixty-five brands of cheap soaps that had erstwhile appeared in plain lettered paper wrappers, came out with coverings emblazoned with all the tints and hues of the spectrum and, to boot, with eye-popping chromos of lovely hussies in the altogether, young widows being chased down the boulevards by Senators in top hats, satyrs taking advantage of moonlit nights, midinettes standing on iron-grillings with the wind blowing their petticoats heavenward, and other such inspiriting spectacles. In a short time, too, the long-standing and unromantic labels, most of them consisting simply of the manufacturers' names, disappeared and in their places were duly beheld such provocative designations as "Lovers' Kiss," "Perfect Passion," "Nuit d'Amour," "Don Juan's Delight," etc. And with these changes, there came a change as well in the perfuming of the soaps, for where formerly they were not much more nostril-massaging than nigger gin, they now began to give out the smells of musk, tuberoses and similarly puissant fauna and flora. The change worked like magic. The French, until now almost as hostile to soap as to the Hun, found themselves attracted to it as they had never before been, and sales began to mount steadily. The circus colors, the exciting pictures, the pretty names and the irresistible empyreumas had turned the trick. And another feather went into the cap of French diplomacy.

§ 8

The National Anathema.—Whatever the backwardness of the Republic in the other fine arts, its sovereignty in the matter of cussing is incontestible. The progress that has been made in this department of research during the last fifteen or twenty years must be the envy and despair of the European and Asiatic nations. Although exact figures are not at hand, it is safe to say that never has swearing been brought to such a height of perfection as in the United States at the present day.

With rare ingenuity, aided and abetted by inventions in the vernacular, the American has developed his vocabulary of imprecation to a point where it boasts at least a dozen synonyms for every circumscribed and hence rapidly become impotent cuss expression of the foreigner. The Englishman, for example, when a taxi driver cozens him out of twopence or when a débutante upsets her Yorkshire pudding upon his boiled shirt, is limited to a "bloody" or a "blarsted." The German, in a relative situation, is able to relieve his feelings only with a *"Donnerwetter"* or a *"Gott verdammte,"* and the Frenchman with a *"bibiche"* or the *mot de* Cambronne. Consider, on the other hand, the high virtuosity of the American. The repertoire for such an occasion includes at least forty different and distinct dismaying verbal pasties, ranging all the way from the obvious invocations of the Deity and injunctions of a biological and procreative nature to allusions to color and race, zoölogical genealogy, the antonym for *caput equum*, vermin, sexual irregularity, moral obliquity, affinity with the cockroach, and inability to distinguish between anatomy and a hole in the ground. Taking a single example, consider the Frenchman and the American in the presence of the soul-satisfying necessity of bestowing objurgation upon a fellow whose stupidity is offensive and unbearable. When the Frenchman, also calling upon the vernacular, has issued an *"andouille,"* a *"boule,"* a *"gnaif,"* a *"godichon,"* a *"gogo,"* a *"hure,"* a *"mange-crottin,"* a *"carrelet empaillé,"* or a *"tuile"*—a sizeable arsenal, God knows!—he is through; all that is left for him to do, if his feelings are not yet relieved, is either to spit upon the fellow, which is very impolite, or go out and get drunk. The American, on the contrary, even if he be of inefficient salivary glands and a teetotaler, has enough verbal powder at his command to blow the poor fellow up completely. He begins with "bonehead" and proceeds, *seriatim*, through the 122 synonyms for "bonehead," such as mush-head, thick-head, marble-top, stone-head, cement-nut, cobble-bean, ivory-pate, etc., etc.; he goes then to "jackass" and proceeds, *seriatim*, through its fifty-six synonyms such as "mule," "mutt," "sap," "boob," "simp," "goopher," "goat," etc., etc.; he now has recourse to no less than 365 phrases like "the cat's rheumatism," "the rhinoceros' ear-muffs" and "the snake's gall-stones"; he turns, after a deep inhalation, to animadversions—numbering 137—upon the fellow's moral derelictions as the cause of his present weak-mindedness; he moves thereafter to a wholesale derogation in terms of twenty-eight separate and distinct species of insects; and then finally brings up with a fortissimo flourish of forty-five observations upon the fellow's dubious birth, youthful indiscretions, defective physical cleanliness and relationships to various specimens of offal.

In any given situation, the American, when it comes to a matter of the *mot brut,* is a walking Roget. Put him up against a foreigner, the Italian included,—even, indeed, the Chinese with his almost matchless *"Tsao ni hsie pan tsa"*—and the latter is in the position of a duellist armed with a wooden hatpin. The native slang has been instrumental in providing the citizen of These States with a battery of vituperative guns that has no equal in the modern civilized word. But slang has not been the sole source. The American, ever first in progress, has given the matter of cussing as much serious attention as he has given the more mechanical devices of daily physical comfort. He has performed endless laboratory experiments with the established cuss words and expressions and has made a dozen grow where only one grew before. Some Americans, indeed, have made a study of the subject their life's work. There is a man in Chicago, for example, an estimable and talented pedant, who has over a period of twenty-five years devoted himself to the compilation of a dictionary of synonyms for the fundamental motif-terms of swearing. There is another in Seattle who has spent an equal period in research work relative to the verbal inventions of American longshoremen, cowboys, sailors and evangelical clergymen. One of these days we shall have a standard reference work on the subject. Better than anything else will it provide the world with an illuminating portrait of *Homo Americanus* on the daily warpath.

§ 9

Christianity in the Far East.—The Anglo-Saxon campaign to bring light to the heathen Orient, pursued with ferocity for years, has been the subject of much debate pro and con. We have had figures showing the number of infidel Chinese who have been converted to Christianity and still other figures showing the number who, directly after they have been converted and have got free Bibles printed on stock thin enough to make excellent cigarette paper, have gone back to Buddha and rice wine. We have had the reports of missionaries as to the number of Chinamen who have given up native opium and the reports of others as to the number who, having given it up, have taken up imported hasheesh instead. We have learned from Y. M. C. A. officials the number of Chinese gentlemen who have substituted handball and a course in book-keeping for fan-tan and from transplanted San Francisco bordello *régisseurs* the number who have, in turn, given up handball and book-keeping for automatic pianos with nickel slots and former burlesque girls.

From such reports, pleasantly contradictory as they are, we can gain no adequate idea as to the exact degree in which the Anglo-Saxon has succeeded in civilizing the Chinese. But we can, I believe, gain a very fetching idea from the very best source from which such an idea may be obtained, to wit, from a study of advertisements of Anglo-Saxon merchants which appear in the Chinese journals, which reflect the inculcated tastes of the modern Chinese, and which show more or less precisely the specific nature of the phenomena with which the cause of Western civilization has been furthered. I have before me eight Chinese gazettes,

148

all rich in advertisements of the following instruments of Anglo-Saxon evangelical Kultur: 1. the Orthophonic Victrola; 2. the Yale lock; 3. U. B. Beer, "always pure, always sparkling, always fresh"; 4. spare parts for Citroën cars; 5. Mustard and Company's filing cabinets; 6. Moyer, Powell and Company's voiles and Summer dress goods; 7. Sullivan's carpets; 8. M. Levy's patent cigarette cases; 9. the Union Insurance Society's insurance policies for motor cars; 10. Hirschbrunner and Company, Gent's Tailors; 11. the Whitelaw three-part bedstead; 12. the "Handie" folding scissors and the "Openeezie" penknife; 13. the "Quick-strop" razor strop; 14. the "Bungalow" toilet set; 15. B. V. D.'s; 16. Pommery and Greno Champagne, Caldbeck, MacGregor and Company, Ltd., Agents; 17. Colorite American straw hats; 18. the Pathé-Baby motion picture camera; 19. the "One" Egyptian cigarette; 20. Paris sunshades; 21. Scott's cheroots; 22. "Baby's Own Tablets" for infantile indigestion, constipation, colic, diarrhœa, simple fever, worms and teething pains; 23. Rudolph Valentino and Agnes Ayres in "The

Sheik," and Conrad Nagel and May McAvoy in "Grumpy"; 24. Socony Oils; 25. Michelin tires; 26. Addressograph machines; 27. French assorted chocolates; 28. Maroulis Cavalla cigarettes; 29. D. A. Painter and Company's roll-top desks; 30. Sims and Company's window shades; 31. Miss Punnett's (lounge of Grand Hotel des Wagons Lits) pearl and crystal necklaces and tanned, sanitary furs; 32. E. Clemann's wristwatches and loving cups; 33. "Pinkettes" for halitosis; 34. Crystal Table Waters; 35. Miller Cord Tires; 36. Dr. Williams' Pink Pills for the complexion; 37. Johnny Walker whiskey; 38. "Wearwell" cashmere socks; 39. the "Resteezy" bed; 40. Ranolite baby carriages; 41. "Valyu" cruets; 42. How to learn the saxophone in six lessons; 43. Brambury's "Excelsis" hair restorer; 44. Goldfarb and Company's Nose-Straightener; 45. Fit-Well sport coats; 47. the Indestructible collar-button; 48. the novels of Sax Rohmer; 49. Economy radio sets; 50. Dewar's Scotch whiskey; 51. Mexican Sun-ray diamonds; 52. Imperial eyelash liquid dressing; and 53. the Successo bust-developer.

Glory hallelujah! Amen.

§ 10

The Sandwich.—One of the tableaux that engages the interest of the student of the modern American scene is the sandwich wave that has latterly engulfed the country. As little as a half dozen years ago the sandwich industry occupied a position of relatively small importance in the American economic and social history; today it has become one of the leading industries of the land, taking precedence over soda-water, candy, chewing-gum and the *Saturday Evening Post*. I am told that the companies that supply sandwiches to the drug-stores alone in various large and small cities are making fortunes. That there are sandwich-restaurant impresarios in every city in the country who—up to a few years ago poor little delicatessen dealers—now wear dinner jackets every evening and own Packard Sixes, we already know. In New York City alone there are 5,682 shops that specialize in sandwiches, and every one of them is prosperous. In Philadelphia, there are 726; in Chicago, 2,312; in San Francisco, 631; in Cleveland, 442; in Boston, 919; in St. Louis, 802; in the small town

151

of Altoona, Pa., 30 as this is written. In addition to these specializing delicatessen and the drug and candy stores, the regular better-class restaurants that, seven or eight years ago, did not deign to list the lowly sandwich on their menus, have been compelled to surrender to the demands of public taste and presently offer a comprehensive catalogue.

What is responsible for the comparatively sudden and enormous popularity of a victual that, readily within the memory of all of us, was confined very largely to the family pantry and the proletarian back room of Emil Humpfvogel's saloon? One can't dismiss this popularity as a fad; the roots of the thing go much deeper. Exactly what the reason is, I do not know, but I venture a guess. To argue that the popularity of the sandwich is due to its low price seems to me to be nonsense. The sandwich has gone up in price proportionately with all other food-stuffs. Even an ordinary drug-store sandwich today costs fifteen or twenty cents, and in the specialty bureaux sandwiches come as high as a dollar and a half. A simple cheese sandwich that used to sell for a nickel now brings forty cents in a restaurant; a ham sandwich, that used to sell for the same amount, now brings a similar price; a club sandwich, the aristocrat of sandwiches in our youth and reserved only for gala Saturday nights, that used to cost thirty-five cents, now invades the money-pocket to the degree of a dollar or more. It is not the price of the sandwich that brings in the trade, but, I venture, the circumstance that it has shown an imagination and development unknown in the instance of any other native comestible. The sandwich has been brought to a state of variety and virtuosity that has made the standard dishes of the conventional American table seem excessively dull and no longer palatably interesting. There is not a taste that the sandwich, in one form or another, cannot today gratify. The shop-girl and the lady of fashion, the day-laborer and the Brillat-Savarin alike are able to tickle their respective fancies with it.

A glance at the restaurant cards of the early 'nineties shows the sandwich only in its elementary state. There were then, I find, simply Schweitzer cheese sandwiches, ham sandwiches, sardine sandwiches, liverwurst sandwiches, egg sandwiches, corned beef sandwiches, roast beef sandwiches and tongue sandwiches—a measly repertoire, one will note, of just eight. Today, there are no less than 1,546 different recorded kinds of sandwiches. I list a few; the few will suggest their manifold kin. There are obtainable at the present moment—and new species are being added daily—tuna fish sandwiches, chicken salad sandwiches, cream cheese and Bar le Duc sandwiches, tomato and grated clove sandwiches, lobster and cole slaw sandwiches, grated egg, ham and onion, or so-called Western sandwiches, caviar and egg sandwiches, snail sandwiches, watermelon and pimento sandwiches, the so-called combination sandwiches to the number of 237, peanut-butter sandwiches, truffle sandwiches, crab-meat sandwiches, fried oyster sandwiches, vegetable salad sandwiches, Bermuda onion and parsley sandwiches, celery-root sandwiches, turbot sandwiches, beefsteak sandwiches, sandwiches bordelaise, fruit salad sandwiches, mushroom sandwiches, shrimp sandwiches, Spanish embuchado sandwiches, gallego and bilbao sandwiches, sausage sandwiches lyonnaise, aspic of foie-gras sandwiches, liver and bacon sandwiches, kidney sandwiches, spaghetti sandwiches, sweet pepper sandwiches, guava preserve sandwiches, fig sandwiches, red snapper roe sandwiches, shad roe sandwiches, Mojarras sandwiches, stuffed olive sandwiches, headcheese sandwiches, terrapin sandwiches, salmon sandwiches, salmi of duck sandwiches, mousse of lamb sandwiches, pig's knuckle and horseradish sandwiches, hot turkey with candied sweet potatoes sandwiches, bacon and fried egg sandwiches, six layer club sandwiches, hamburger sandwiches, anchovy sandwiches, tartare sandwiches, lake sturgeon with India relish sandwiches, hard boiled egg, lettuce and tomato sandwiches, imported salami sandwiches, spiced beef sandwiches, smoked whitefish with Russian dressing sandwiches, chow-chow sandwiches, minced chicken and deviled egg sandwiches, grated milk chocolate with peanut butter sandwiches, chopped turkey with chopped almonds and grated olives sandwiches, walnut fudge and cream cheese sandwiches, celery with chopped green peppers and mayonnaise sandwiches, date, raisin and chopped nut sandwiches, corned beef and cole slaw sandwiches, grilled bacon and hard boiled egg sandwiches, roast pork and candied sweet potato sandwiches, three-decker roast beef, ham and cheese sandwiches, pickled herring sandwiches, asparagus tip sandwiches, deep sea scollop sandwiches, and so on *ad infinitum.*

The variety of foods at the average American restaurant outside of New York City, large or small, expensive or cheap, is on the other hand relatively scanty. One need only compare the usual restaurant bill-of-fare with even a drug-store sandwich bulletin board to appreciate how much more readily the gastronomic fancy of the average person may be gratified by the latter, humble as it is. The sandwich has beaten out the rest of the restaurant table for the same reason that the phonograph has beaten the music-box: the former plays a thousand tunes, where the best the latter could manage was a half dozen.

§ 11

House Organs.—One of the most amusing consequences of the recent and sudden itch for Kultur amongst us is to be observed in the many little magazines, brochures and pamphlets published monthly by various commercial organizations and known to the trade as house organs. In earlier days, when bankers were content to be bankers and didn't seek to constitute themselves authorities on the opera, drama, painting and all the other arts and when steam pump manufacturers were satisfied to be steam pump manufacturers and didn't wish to impress their neighbors, to boot, with their literary talents, these house organs devoted themselves intelligently and solely to the immediate business of the organizations. But today it is a rare booklet of the species that does not interrupt its disquisition on the manufacture of wall paper or the wonders of a certain brand of bug-sprayer with a tasty essay on Montaigne, an appreciation of the genius of Rachmaninoff or a page of epigrams showing the wall paper and bug-sprayer trade what La Bruyère and Anatole France thought of women.

§ 12

The Revolt of Youth.—The most intelligent editorial that I have read in some time is just about two and a half inches in length and appears not in one of the august organs of public opinion but in a magazine published by the students of the little university at Bloomington, Indiana. It bears the title, "The Revolt of Youth," and this is its essence: "The great majority of the youth of this university were surprised and flattered when Dr. Stephen S. Wise recently announced to them that they were in revolt. Seven or eight, certainly not more than a dozen, boys on the campus are in revolt, but they are by no means representative of the student body. There is a great deal of hokum about the youth movement all over the world. To hear speakers like Dr. Wise, one would think that every person under the age of thirty is a walking Vesuvius, when as a matter of fact the circle of progressive free-thinkers is very small."

The notion that the student bodies in our universities and colleges are in a state of seething rebellion and that no professor with so many as two white hairs in his whiskers is safe from derision and flying ink-pots has long struck anyone acquainted with the true state of affairs as just a

158

bit comical. About five or six years ago, a few obstreperous boys were kicked out of as many colleges for printing pieces in the college papers or for getting up in class-room and proclaiming, with that bravado chronic to sophomores since the first university opened its doors, that all professors were *ipso facto* idiots, that none of them knew enough to come in when it rained, and that all of them should be bound up in potato sacks and thrown into the nearest lake. Out of this circumstance, the like of which any middle-aged university man easily recalls as having happened more or less regularly for the last thirty years, there sprang the theory, assiduously nourished by editorial writers hard up for ideas, that these few boys were typical of student bodies as a whole all over the country and, as a corollary, that the youth of the land was through with the old and established order and was already trying on the coat of Trotsky and the pantaloons of Lenin. The simple truth of the matter, of course, was and is that these miniature Branns and sapling Voltaires no more represented or represent the great body of college students than a couple of loud-mouthed congressmen from the store-pie States represent the great body of the American people.

The so-called intellectual revolt in our colleges is not a revolt at all. Investigate it at first hand and all that you find it to be is exactly what it has been ever since—almost three decades ago it is now—I, with other boys like me, first stuck pipes in our hat-bands, buttoned only the lower buttons of our coats and so became members of the Athenian grove. In those days—and my father used to tell me it was the same in his—there were, as now, always three or four of us bumptious cerebrals who thought that we knew everything, and that no one else knew anything, and that any professor who didn't discern our remarkable genius in a flash was by way of being a profound ass. I hope that I do not lower myself too much in your, to say nothing of my present own, estimation when I confide to you that on one occasion, back in the early nineteen hundreds, I myself came very near being booted out of college for just such a quasi-radical revolt as currently entertains and deludes the editorial philosophers. It all amounted, as it amounts

160

today, to nothing. The student bodies then, as the student bodies now, were and are no more in revolt than the populace of Old Point Comfort or Palm Beach. What is mistaken for the sign and symptom of intellectual revolt is merely the suppressed and natural youthful desire on the part of certain college boys to upset·trolley-cars, ring door-bells, steal signs and trip up policemen and, finding that desire ungratified by reason of one inhibition or another, to take it out in raising a little pseudo-radical hell. I have gone carefully over the list of college boys who, since 1919, have figured as leaders of the undergraduate revolution. In that list I find ten outstanding names. What are these Tom Paines, these Kosciuszkos, these Bolivars and Huxleys doing today? They are still youths, let us remember, and, I repeat, what are they doing? Three of them are working quietly and obediently in their fathers' businesses, to wit, the manufacture of window screens, the selling of automobile tires and the writing of life insurance policies; one is helping his pa run a chicken farm in Missouri; two are humdrum reporters on newspapers, covering six-day bicycle races, the birth of triplets in

the Bronx and John D. Rockefeller's golf game;
two are teaching in provincial high schools; one is
writing hack fiction for the shop-girl magazines;
and the tenth, unquestionably the one potentially
talented fellow in the lot, is doing book reviews,
and good ones, for the literary journals. Of such
are the brave Continentals of the insurrection.

§ 13

The Court of Justice.—If I were to be invested the
Mussolini of These States tomorrow, with full
power to exercise my sagacity in whatever direction I deemed that exercise necessary, the first
thing that I should do would be to line up all
lawyers who demand that witnesses answer questions with a simple *yes* or *no* and shoot them.
Shrewd shysterism has never, with nonsensical procedure on its side and with the court's consequent
necessary concurrence, evolved a more obfuscating
and transparently unfair technique of chicane.
That it is impossible, save in a purely superficial
manner and to a purely hypothetical degree, to
answer certain questions in the absolute affirmative
or negative, everyone knows. Yet the prestidigita-

tion of the law permits the buncombe a free course, to the embarrassment and confusion of honestly inclined witnesses and to the subversion of justice. A witness in a murder case was, on a certain night, sitting in a room with the window closed and the blinds drawn. He could hear the sound of water dripping against the panes. "Was it raining that night—answer *yes* or *no?*" demands the prosecutor. "It sounded as if it was," replies the witness, accurately enough. Whereupon the shyster gets as indignantly red in the face as a pair of fireman's underdrawers, pounds his fist upon the table and yells his demand for a simple affirmative or negative. "Did you mean what you wrote in this part of the letter—answer *yes* or *no?*" insists another shyster. The witness, intelligibly, may not conceivably recall to just what degree he meant what he wrote; he may have been a bit honestly doubtful himself, since his mind at the moment he wrote was not entirely clear. He tries to explain that doubt in a forthright manner. Whereupon the shyster tears at his collar as if it were a luscious pig's-knuckle, glowers at the poor fellow on the stand and demands that he lie by resorting

163

to an equivocally definite reply. Almost any trial
is full of such hamstringing. Hardly a witness,
though honest as the day is long, but is not sub-
jected to this, the unfairest and dirtiest device
known to the administration of theoretical justice.

§ 14

The Country's Need.—It was the late Marshall of
Indiana, then Vice-President of the Republic, who,
as I recall, observed that what the country needed
most was a good five-cent cigar. While I do not
for a moment wish to deny a measure of truth
to the estimable Marshall's observation, the fact
remains that it was little more than a very fetching epigram and without that complete soundness
of statement that one looks for in Vice-Presidents.
A good five-cent cigar has been an utter impossibility since McKinley's time; it remains but a
memory of happy days long gone; it is out of the
question in these later years because of the high
price of labor, high taxation and what not. Marshall might just as rationally have said that what
the country needed most was a good twenty-five
dollar blue serge suit. But there is something that

164

the country needs badly and that it feasibly and very easily can get and can have. And that is a three-dollar bill.

With the gradual increase in the cost of things since the late war broke out, the dollar, as we unhappily know, ceased to be a dollar in its erstwhile sense. It no longer could buy what it once did, nor, for that matter, could two dollars. The two-dollar bill, indeed, became so useless for purposes of general daily commerce that the government stopped printing it. And with what result? With the result that today there is no intermediate bill between the one-dollar and five-dollar bill. Yet the average man often finds that his purchases in a score of directions run to an amount between the two sums, and it is a well-known fact that hardly ever has anyone change for a five-dollar bill. What is worse, the purchaser himself seldom has change to cover the situation. He may have a number of five- or ten-dollar bills; he may have some loose silver change; but it is a rare day that he has a sufficient number of one-dollar bills. I venture to guess that if you were to accost the next dozen men you meet on the street and ask each of

them how many one-dollar bills he had in his
pocket, you would find not more than three at
most out of the twelve who had more than two such
bills about their persons. A three-dollar bill would
be easily changed; it would speed up trade; it
would lighten the burdens of countless men; and
it would prove a boon to a country at present beset by the intricacies of the problem of getting
change without considerable delay, hard feeling
and loud damning.

§ 15

Psycho-Osteopathy.—It is passing strange that the
moral police of the country have thus far overlooked those chiropractors of the sub-conscious
who begin to flourish in every community that
boasts so much as a brick railroad station and a
gilt movie parlor, and whose occult enterprises
constitute what is undoubtedly one of the high-
voltage engines of sinfulness amongst us. I allude,
of course, to the profession of psycho-analysis, an
art that has summoned to it as professors such a
body of quacks and charlatans as has not been
heard of since Christian Science first got under

full steam. There are, plainly enough, a few professional practitioners of the Freudian pathology who are competent men, but the great majority of fellows that one finds ploughing the field in search of easy pickings are simply so many illicit emotion plumbers, as devious and crooked as their colleagues in the gold brick, shell game and oil stock businesses.

The Freud-Jung-Adler psycho-pathological science has gradually passed out of the hands of those best fitted to understand and further interpret it—of those for whom it was designed—and has become simply a playing-ground for shrewd mountebanks. The latter have had an easy time of it, as the rank and file of half-wits have assimilated only the superficial elements of the doctrines and are hence ready and eager to swallow at one gulp anything that is told them. Many of these mountebanks do no actual harm, as their activities are confined to such absurdities as the confection of novels in which a bull-fighter afraid of cows is cured of his fear complex by being forced to eat a two-foot rump steak, and German moving pictures in which phallic symbolism is subtly indicated by a flash of the Kochelbräu chimney. But there are others, and they outnumber the rest by twenty to one, who are breaking up more homes, assisting more greatly in the spread of muco-purulent inflammation and raising more hell generally than all the whiskey ever made in Kentucky or all the literature ever produced in France. I allude, it must be obvious, to the women's club lecturers and, more especially and directly, to those doctors and dentists who have lost their licenses and set up shop in the side-streets as psycho-analysts, and to the considerable company of fortune-tellers, osteopaths, phrenologists and Italian counts who, observing the ample supply of impressionable suckers, have closed their old places of business, sprouted whiskers and followed suit.

The procedure of this light-fingered gentry is simple. The women's clubs, to begin at the beginning, have long since tired of sitting through lectures on Jacob Wassermann under the delusion that it was August the orator on the platform was going to talk about. They have rebelled, as well, against sitting through two hour lectures on Cabell for a measly five minutes' confidential disquisition on the nature of Jurgen's implements of war. Deeply as it pains me to say it, it yet has always been plain to anyone acquainted with these women's clubs that what they really wanted was a little hot stuff carefully and politely wrapped in a literary, philosophical or scientific cloak, and that the payment of dues always fell off alarmingly when the lecturers engaged by the secretaries did not come up to expectations. These secretaries, who are customarily the only women in the clubs who get paid for their services, were not long in seeing which way the wind was blowing and in feeling the ground gradually give way under their jobs, and they presently removed their intellectual spectacles and got busy. Appreciating that many more lectures on the style of Georges Duhamel and the iambic pentapody of Salvador Novo would find them back at their old, less glamorous posts in department stores or teaching school, they promptly cast about them for a means to get the old girls to continue sending in their cheques, and they were quick to find it in the lecturers on psychoanalysis. These gentlemen, of whom there are so many available that the lecture bureaux have to hire special clerks to keep them in line, could be relied upon to give a good dirty show under cover. Under the guise of informing the women's clubs on the scientific aspects of the Freudian alectry-omancy, it was an easy matter for them to go safely into hitherto forbidden territory, to the huge delight and satisfaction of the lady scientists out front and the secretaries.

The *modus operandi* of the gentlemen was and is readily recognizable. They begin with a lot of harmless whiffle on such relatively innocuous matters as the nutritional instinct, intellectual elaboration of instinct, the conflict between social urge and individual craving, anxiety as a protective cloak against asocial tendencies, narcotomania, Wagner-Jauregg's observations on the infantile root of the tendency to steal, and a couple of illustrations of children setting fire to chicken-coops—to the polite boredom of the assembled girls. They then move cautiously ahead and discourse, a bit more easily and with fewer pulls at their whiskers, upon such subjects as the Œdipus complex, the Electra complex and the more discreet cases cited in other

directions by Wimmer, Weinberg, Leppmann and
Duboisson—and the girls begin to prick up their
ears. The lecturers, gaining confidence, now move
on to Janet's theory of dromomania, with its impulse to flee home and husband, the significance of
dreams about conflagrations, the sexual symbolism
of sleep-walking and the dangers of repression—
and the girls are now leaning so far forward in
their seats that the ushers have to stand guard lest
they fall out. Then, after a cough or two, the lecturers pick up bag and baggage and move directly
into the metaphysical boudoir.

The lecture over, the girls duly rush back to
congratulate the speaker (and to find out covertly
how strong his grip is), disperse to their homes to
nag their husbands—and to consider the lay of the
land. Thus meditating, they conclude that all is
not well with them and that it would be meet for
them to consult, as soon as possible, one of the
local psycho-analysts. The latter they have no
more trouble in locating than formerly they had
in the case of fortune-tellers. A suave fellow, they
find him to be, with the voice and manner of a
stock company actor, with a consultation chamber

soothingly dim and with perhaps some Turkish smell-powder burning in a corner. To this professor, they address their woes and beseech advice. The professor glances at the size of their diamonds, learnedly strokes his Van Dyke and deliberates. A dozen or so negligible questions follow; there is a laborious and copious taking of data; there is a measure of punditical ear-stroking; and the professor—if the diamonds strike him as big enough—informs the fair one that hers is a difficult case demanding much study, and will she return again in three or four days' time. (If the diamonds are deficient, it is a matter of ten dollars and goodbye.) At the expiration of the stipulated period, the clothes-horse shows up again and the professor goes through the same rigmarole. Four or five visits will be necessary; the client presents a problem—but, let her rest assured, he will solve it. Now, as the client knows precisely what she wishes to be told—and as the pseudo-psycho-analyst knows that she knows—all that the latter need do is to slick up his beard with a little more bear-grease and bide his time against a sufficiently sizeable fee. At length, feeling that the customer has been properly impressed with his stupendous ratiocinations and is ready to be nicked to the limit, the charlatan confides to her that, as a result of his findings, he believes the trouble with her to lie in the direction of a suppressed libido. The cure for her ills, psychic and physical, is, he tells her, to be found in a release of her throttled desires. The customer, obviously, is immensely pleased with the professor's sagacity in discerning the true nature of her malaise; gladly remunerates him for his wisdom; and departs. And the moment she departs, another American home is due for disruption and another American husband for horns.

The number of women, young and old, who have been dispatched on fleshly errands and been convinced by the psycho-analyst frauds of the moral legitimacy of their quests cannot accurately be determined, but it must run well up into the tens of thousands. Many of these women are of the sort who would not indulge their emotional whims save they honestly believed such an indulgence to be warranted by their deep psychic and physical needs, in other words, save they believed that they

173

had a scientific justification for their peccadilloes, and with this justification the Freudian fakers provide them. Nor are married women whose husbands, to put it euphemistically, devote too much time to their business, the only class of females who fall for the sexual necromancy of these humbugs. . . . There was a day when men used to hang around stage-doors. Today, you will find the same men, bent on the same mission, hanging around outside the offices of the Freudian practitioners. They are the psycho-analytical Johns of 1927.

§ 16

Romance and America.—The pathetic lack of and longing for romantic glamour in the United States in these years of the Twentieth Century are clearly impressed upon us in the circumstances attending the death, not long ago, of the moving picture actor, Valentino. Laugh at the spectacle as one may, the fact remains that Valentino was the one figure who had succeeded in capturing the romantic fancy of American women since the day of Richmond Pearson Hobson, twenty-five years before. For a quarter of a century, that is, there was no man to bounce the imagination of the bulk of American females and to present himself to them in the light of a resplendent hero and lover. To the majority of men, of course, there was approximately as much romantic glamour to Valentino as there is to a plate of ravioli, and as for Hobson, for all his greater engagement with masculine adventure, there was not so very much more. But, to women condemned to lives in the company of mesh underwear manufacturers, stock salesmen and shirt clerks, there was a great deal, and reasonably. For Valentino and Hobson had about them that thing which beguiles the fancy of women, and which their American husbands and beaux lack, to wit— and for want of a better phrase—romantic insolence. That the one was a mere film posturer and the other simply a play-actor without greasepaint only goes to demonstrate more fully the poverty in the native materials of rhapsody.

Valentino and Hobson are merely the symbols of a greater and more important deficiency in American color and the craving therefor. In no other country in the world is the national palette so lacking in hues. Abroad, the proletariat has its kings, queens, princes, dictators and generals dressed up like circus horses to inflame and enchant its fancy. The American has only a President in a business suit and a Vice-President who chews tobacco. Abroad, the commoners have their legendary Joans of Arc and their Cids to keep alive the spirit of their flower-day fêtes. The American has only, in comparison, his Barbara Frietchie, forgotten with the school-room poem, and Admiral Dewey, who shouldn't have put that house in his wife's name. Yet how pathetically the poor American strives for the superficial glamour that doesn't exist! He engauds himself with Mystic Shriner regalia in the attempt to delude himself that he is a gallant crusader to the Holy Land. He adorns his derby hat with ostrich plumes and straps a tin sword to his side by way of making himself believe that he is a knight out of heroic times. He makes a hero out of a politician who got on a horse with hundreds of guns behind him, rode up a hill about as high as the grave of an Exalted Mogul of the Moose and chased a dozen starving Spaniards down the other side. He declares a half holiday and yells himself hoarse in patriotic excitement when a German girl and a Danish woman, astutely carrying American flags, come home after swimming the English Channel. Let those American men who snicker at foolish women for making a hero out of the good-looking Italian Valentino on the theory that he was a champion Casanova reserve a snicker equally as robust for that considerable portion of their own foolish sex which, a few years before, made a hero out of a good-looking Frenchman on the theory that he was a champion prize-fighter.

§ 17

Railroad Travel.—Returning a short time ago from a trip back and forth across the continent, and after having whiled away the journey perusing the *de luxe* literature got out by the various railroad companies eulogizing their own great gifts in making rail travel lovely and comfortable beyond words, I bring myself to wonder why the companies do not leave off trying to impress their customers with fresh mountain trout, pants-pressers, manicure girls and bound copies of the

177

latest *Saturday Evening Post,* and hire a capable construction engineer (or whatever he elects to call himself) to figure out a way to lessen the infernal racket made by the car wheels. Railway travel in America is indistinguishable from riding in a perambulating boiler-factory. There may be a measure of comfort in American train washrooms, compartments, dining cars and even barber shops, but it all disappears from the consciousness because of the accompaniment of terrific rumble and din. In Europe, one may ride in a railway train with one's ears at peace. Here, it is like having swallowed an orchestra playing "Feuersnot."

Although an amateur at mechanics and barely able to tell the difference between a turbine engine and an electric fan, I am yet of the opinion that railroad travel might be made a somewhat quieter phenomenon than it presently is. All the superficial comforts installed by the companies cannot make up for the torture suffered from the noise that currently batters the human tympanum. Might not the floors of the cars be made soundproof? Or wouldn't it be possible for someone who knows about such things so to set the wheels against the cars, and in turn against the rails, that much of the present racket would disappear? If the report of an exploding revolver can be silenced, why can't a car-wheel? We are told that American railway cars are necessarily overly heavy because of the distances and topographical difficulties they are called upon to surmount. Yet the distance and the nature of the road-bed between, say, New York and Philadelphia are not so greatly different from those between Southampton and London and still the American trains make twenty times more uproar than the English. A railway coach climbing up and down the Western mountain country may justifiably make all the hubbub it wants to, but I can see no reason for one moving between Newark and Elizabeth, New Jersey, making an equal one. If engines are changed, why can't coaches be changed and lighter ones be substituted for rides across the plains and flat-lands? It would not take more than a few minutes to make such changes, and the tremendous addition in peace and comfort would amply repay the traveler—and the company—for the trouble and inconvenience. Better still, I repeat the suggestion that the railroad companies save the money they are presently wasting on handsome brochures boasting of the "gentlemen's club" nature of their special trains, and spend it on some fellow who may be able to devise a way to make them sound rather more like a gentleman's club and less like the Battle of Bull Run.

§ 18

A Vanished Institution.—Thirty years ago, there was hardly a well-to-do American home whose parlor was not embellished, in one of its corners, with a glass-front piece of furniture known as a curio cabinet. It usually rested on ten-inch legs and contained three or four shelves whereon reposed, presumably for the edification of the family and its more favored guests, a variety of small articles collected at considerable pains and expense, and theoretically of rare value. One beheld small ivory elephants, little Dresden china shepherdesses, dimes with the Lord's Prayer engraved upon them, Columbian half dollars, Chinese lucky stones, miniature clocks set into walnuts, tiny thermometers affixed to china apricots, small chips of Lookout Mountain, samples of coral, pieces of polished granite, the usual bogus autographs of Abraham Lincoln, silk programs of the Philadelphia Centennial, cloisonné tea-cups, grandfathers' watch-fobs, miniature ivory skulls, small fourteen-karat gold cats' heads with rhinestone eyes, medals won by mythical great-uncles and an assortment of similar odds and ends ranging all the way from hand-painted medallions of Napoleon Bonaparte to letters from William McKinley, discreetly left in their envelopes, declining invitations to serve as godfather to the families' babies. What has become of these cabinets, and of the opulent treasures they once contained? Not one is visible in the land today. Their place, I venture to guess, has been taken over by phonographs, Dr. Eliot's five-foot shelves, cellarettes, radio sets, Japanese growing-gardens and the complete works of Michael Arlen. Thus has the country gone to hell!

NO. 18

§ 1

The Question of Repeal.—One can't fail to look with a humorous pity upon those deluded souls who are confident that the Eighteenth Amendment will be repealed during their time on earth and that once again the lithograph capricornus, the free lunch, the basket of pretzels, the soaped mirror, the white apron, the dish of cloves, the brightly shined foot-rail and the succulent dill-pickle will appear to gladden the street-corner. Politicians may change all they want to, but so long as human nature doesn't change the Eighteenth Amendment stands no more chance of being stricken from the national legal bible than the Thirteenth. In order to get rid of Prohibition, an immense amount of wampum would be needed to bribe, buy up, shanghai and blackmail the dry members of Congress, and such an amount will never be forthcoming during our lifetime. And for a very simple reason.

Every American who is well enough off in worldly goods to contribute so much as even a measly ten dollars to any cause, or to the cause of the wets in particular, today has all he wants to drink or, if he hasn't, knows where he can get it either simply by lifting the telephone receiver off the hook or walking around the corner to a convenient blind-pig, "club" or restaurant back-room. To persuade this contented fellow to grow sufficiently excited to contribute a nickel toward the alcoholic happiness of men less fortunate than he is, is to have a respect for human nature that centuries of experience with human nature hardly warrant. Since Prohibition doesn't bother him in the least, he has ceased to have any concern with it the one way or the other, and doesn't give a tinker's dam whether the Eighteenth Amendment remains on the books or not. And so, filling up another glass of excellent stuff got in by his bootlegger by way of Canada, Bermuda, Cuba or crooked revenue officers working the North Atlantic coast, he allows the brewers idiotically to campaign themselves to death with negligible amounts of money, the newspaper editorial writers vainly to get writer's cramp and the parched paupers of the country to protest all they want to and go thirsty.

Never since Prohibition went into effect has it been so easy to get good, drinkable liquor at fair prices as it is now. And it is constantly getting easier. On that day when a man with a double Daiquiri cocktail in his fist feels his heart breaking because some yokel out in the farm-tractor belt hasn't got one too, on that day will the Eighteenth Amendment feel the ground under it getting weak. But until that day comes it is founded upon the Gibraltar rock of human nature that doesn't give a hoot so long as it itself has got a bottle hidden in the book-case. Prohibition could doubtless be soon got rid of with a hundred million dollars. But the hundred million necessary dollars, unfortunately or otherwise, happen to be in the pants of men who know of Prohibition only by hearsay.

§ 2

A Sea View of Prohibition.—A study of the smoke-rooms on the trans-Atlantic liners these days offers an enlightening insight into the state of Prohibition currently on tap in the Republic. Crossing back and forth not long ago on two of the largest and most popular of the steamers, the *Mauretania* and the *Olympic*, I noticed that the amount of drinking not only in the smoking-room but also in the dining saloon and restaurant was so small as to be almost indiscernible. Inquiry elicited the news that this lamentable condition of affairs was by no means unusual, that, in point of fact, all the liners were falling off badly in the alcoholic department. The reason, I was told, was a simple one. The American of any means at all, after these half dozen and more years of Volsteadism, has his drinking affairs now so well arranged at home that, where once he booked passage on a steamer to Europe exactly as he would have taken a six days' lease on a brewery, he presently views a ship much in the light of a water-wagon, that is, as a place to get a respite from bibbing, to fill his lungs with salt air, and to ease up the strain on his kidneys.

A few years ago, as everyone knows, the smoke-room of an ocean liner was indistinguishable from a Kentucky distillery. On certain of the smaller ships, indeed, things often got to such a pass, what with the briskness of trade, that the stewards were unable to handle the situation singlehanded and the captain himself had to come down off the bridge to help pull corks. Today, a single steward is amply competent to handle the smoke-room on one of the small passenger vessels, and on such larger boats as the *Mauretania* and *Olympic* a couple are able to manage things with the utmost ease. Even in the Ritz restaurant and veranda café on the latter ship, where erstwhile the popping of corks sounded like the Franco-Prussian War, the wine steward on my voyage had to move about so little in answer to orders that he confided to me, on the third day out, that he was going down to the ship's surgeon to get a liniment to rub on his feet, which were constantly going to sleep.

The revenue from liquor sales on the trans-Atlantic boats has fallen at least fifty per cent in the last three years. The American with enough money in his jeans to travel even at the minimum rate of $250 or $300 now has just as much to drink at home, and almost as good stuff, as he had before Prohibition. He has at last found a satisfactory bootlegger; he no longer has to pay the high prices

for stuff that he had to pay out in the early days
before bootlegging had become well systematized
and proficient; he is no longer tempted to let loose
and get delirium tremens on the high seas simply
because a highball costs sixpence less on board
ship than it does in his own house or across the
street at the speakeasy. The perceptible increase
of traffic on the ships of the American Line, where
no liquor is officially sold, shows which way the
wind is blowing. If things continue to keep on going
as they are, I confidently predict that within another few years all the boats that cater to the American trade will be driven to make up their liquor
deficit by converting their smoking-rooms into moving picture halls and charging the boat-load of temporary teetotalers a stiff admission fee.

§ 3

The Beer Drinker.—One of the commonest arguments against Prohibition is that, with the taking
away of beer, a relatively harmless tipple, erstwhile beer guzzlers have been driven to the imbib-
ing of vastly more deleterious drinks, such as whiskey, gin, etc. While disinclined to give the Prohibi-

tionists any comfort and support, even indirectly, I yet denounce the argument, with its subtle inferences, as buncombe. The genuine beer bibber, that is, the man trained by birth, experience, taste, piety and culture to malt as opposed to the fellow to whom beer is simply a casually acquired taste, is a beer drinker first, last and always, and, if he can't get beer, has no more use for the more puissant *Schnapps* than a German has for crème de cacao. In moments of desolation and despair, he may, true enough, seek solace in whiskey or gin, but his face takes on a wry squint when he downs it; he doesn't like it; it is a sorry makeshift; and nothing will ever get him to like it. If there has ever been a real beer drinker who became a whiskey souse or a gin swiller, his name is unknown to the Munich or Hoboken police. When the authentic *Bierbruder* can't get his seidel, he may call upon the God of his fathers to strike Pussyfoot Johnson, Volstead, Anderson and Wheeler dead, but you will never find him addressing his prayers to the same God for Sandy Macdonald, Dewar, Haig and Haig, or Mr. Gordon.

§ 4

Veritas in Vino.—One of the greatest morsels of balderdash that has come down the ages in proverb form is to the effect that in wine there is truth. In other words, that when a man is in his cups, his speech and action break loose from their erstwhile anchorage of deceit and promptly take on a mantle of veracity and plain dealing. I do not go so far as to say that, in the way of minor detail, a deplorably fried gentleman may not conduct himself in the light of his real nature and character; what I do say is that for one man who is brought to talk and act honestly by contact with ethyl alcohol, there are a hundred who, as a result of the same contact, are converted into even bigger frauds and liars, psychically, physically, rationally, emotionally and every other way, than they were before.

The effect of intoxicating liquids upon the average man, as anyone who takes the trouble to investigate the matter will quickly observe, is to exaggerate in him all his qualities of pretense and simultaneously to reduce in him all his qualities of forthrightness and probity. The only difference between a liar sober and a liar drunk is that, when sober, he lies to deceive others and that, when drunk, he lies to deceive himself. Give the average man half a dozen cocktails and he will promptly proceed to a vast bragging about himself and about his prowess in the courts of Mars, Venus and Babbitt. Sober, he appreciates full well the truth of the fact that his wife can lick him with a single quick left to the jaw, but, oiled, he presents himself as the superior of Mr. Tunney. Sober, he truthfully appreciates that his bank account is overdrawn; pickled, he tosses money hither and thither like the millionaire he would like to be and like to have his friends believe him to be. Sober, he truthfully appreciates that, as a lover, he is on a par with an octogenarian Eskimo; stewed, he recommends himself to whatever fair creature happens to be sitting across the table from him as a cross between the San Francisco earthquake and the Chicago fire.

Alcohol, in short, is the greatest inducer of fake and falsehood known to man. It converts the hard, clear-seeing realist into a moist-eyed romantic, the doltish clam into a pseudo-philosophical chowder,

the mountebank into an even worse mountebank.
If it were the sesame to truth that legend has made
it, the crowded law courts might be cleared in a
few hours simply by keeping a couple of cases of
synthetic gin handy to the witness-box. How the
legend started, it is difficult to make out. A good
guess is that it was floated by some percipient
stews who, realizing that they were actually of
utterly no importance in the world, sought to have
the world accept them at their soused face-value.

§ 5

*Suggested Argument Against Prohibition by the
Authors' League.*—Charles Lamb was such a
boozer that it required the combined efforts of
Coleridge, Hazlitt and Wordsworth, his fellow tip-
plers, to stagger up the stairs with him and get
him into bed. Anatole France, according to his
secretary, Brousson, consumed a quart of cognac
every time he composed a critique and stated that
the only review he ever wrote for the *Temps* which
got him the special commendation of his editor
was a feuilleton he wrote when he was so far gone
that he hadn't the slightest notion he had ever writ-

ten it and didn't recognize it when he saw it in print. Jules Lemaître drank so much that his inamorata, Mme. de Loynes, always brushed his lips with rose-water before allowing him to bestow upon her a loving smack. Ibsen was one of the greatest *Biersäufer* to whom the *Oberkellner* of the Café Luitpold ever vouchsafed a *Grüss Gott,* and Wagner was the delight of the *Wirte* at Beyreuth. Shakespeare, in his earlier years and when he was making the reputation that will never die from man's memory, drank regularly every night he had the money from ten o'clock until two the next morning. Lessing put the breweries of Hamburg on their feet and caused them to pay increased dividends to their stockholders. Stephen Crane knew intimately all the most conspicuous bartenders of his day, and Thomas Hardy, like Conrad before him, keeps a carafe of port handy on the sideboard. When Jack London gave up rum, his writing went to pot.

Swift loved his liquor, as did Chaucer. Rostand's favorite beverage was the white wine of Bordeaux, Château Suduiraut in particular, and Marcel Proust's is Château Climens. Congreve drank a

192

quart of Burgundy every night at dinner, and washed it down with several ponies of brandy. Ambrose Bierce's taste was for straight whiskey, provided only the glasses were big enough, and Nathaniel Hawthorne's was for ale. Sterne was off the stuff only in his unproductive years; the moment he took to ethyl alcohol he produced "Tristram Shandy" and the "Sentimental Journey." William Schwenk Gilbert lived up to the traditions of his middle name, and Fielding wrote "Joseph Andrews" in a mildly pickled state. Sir Charles Napier wrote his one and only book, "War in Syria," after his physician had prescribed a moderate daily use of alcohol after a long and deleterious period of abstinence. Under the assumed name of Dr. Schmidt, Schiller enjoyed the malt of Oggersheim and later of Bauerbach to such a degree that for years afterward he was fretful if any other brew was passed over to him. Byron tried all the tipples of Portugal, Spain, Turkey and Greece, and apparently found them to his liking, and Swinburne's cast-iron stomach is known to history. Dickens was a magnificent stoker of ale; old Sam Johnson's booze chair is familiar to all American

Prohibitionists who have gone to London on Cook's tours; and Oscar Wilde could down six glasses of green Chartreuse or eight of bad brandy without turning a hair.

We come to the present American scene. Who are the outstanding writers in the country today? Dreiser, Cabell, Lewis, Anderson, Hergesheimer, Sandburg, O'Neill—and not one of them, from personal observation, would exactly faint in the presence of a bottle.

A FEW NOTES ON AMERICAN CRITICISM

§ 1

Definition.—Criticism is a technical mastery of the difficult art of keeping unæsthetic personal prejudices out of æsthetic appraisal.

§ 2

The Elephant and the Flea.—"Elephants," wrote Swift, "are always drawn smaller than life, but a flea always larger." In the same way are the stature and bulk of the real artist amongst us relatively diminished by the magnification of the stature and bulk of the inferior artist. The chief fault of American criticism is its warm hospitality to second-rate striving. It often duly appreciates the authentic artist, but detracts from that appreciation by an over-valuation of the dubious artist. Everything that has been written in praise of Cabell has also at one time or another been written in praise of

Donn Byrne. Everything that has been written in praise of Sherwood Anderson and Dreiser has at one time or another been written also of James Oliver Curwood.

§ 3

The American as Critic.—It is the habit of the American critic, whether professional or lay, to answer any question which confounds him by its obvious soundness and unanswerability with a condescending imputation of dubious personal motives on the part of its embarrassing propounder. Unable to reply to the latter's position and argument because of their indubitable integrity, he takes refuge in attributing to the fellow's actions reasons which are palpably dishonest, false and—if he would have his way—humiliating. Thus, when Sinclair Lewis in unmistakable terms declined the Pulitzer prize for his novel, "Arrowsmith," stating as his reason for not accepting it what has long been plainly evident to every self-respecting, sincere and intelligently critical American novelist, answer was made by persons directly and indirectly associated with the award that Lewis was simply up to

196

the antics of a press-agent and was seeking to gain a little free publicity for himself. Thus, again, when Sidney Howard, who was awarded the prize the year before for his play, "They Knew What They Wanted," though he unintelligibly allowed himself to accept it, yet had the good judgment and taste to announce that the committee should properly have given the prize to Eugene O'Neill rather than to himself, it was said that he, too, was simply up to deplorable publicity tricks. And thus, still again, when dignified American artists have declined to accept election to the self-constituted National Institute of Arts and Letters on the ground that they could not quite fathom the nature of an honor which would make them the artistic equals of gentlemen whose contributions to the world of æsthetics consisted chiefly of cheap sex magazine serials, newspaper humor, the organization of Vigilantes to make the lives of German saloon-keepers miserable during the late war, books telling boys how to catch fish in Maine, lectures at girls' finishing schools, moving picture scenarios, nursery rhymes and odes dedicating soldiers' monuments—when, as I say, such dignified craftsmen

have refused so to demean their positions as to
accept initiation into an over-labeled club of the
sort, they have been and are smiled aside with the
animadversion that they are merely out for a bit
of advertising.

Surely, such a species of criticism of an honorable and forthright artist must prove heartily dis-
gusting to any person sufficiently acute to penetrate
its smoke-screen and detect the fundamental un-
certainty, the considerable embarrassment and the
weak attempt to support its misgivings that lie behind. Yet, for all the contemptible cheapness and
stabs in the back that this critical attitude indulges
in, such is the nature of the average American that
he actually believes it to be above-board and honest.
To attribute snide personal motives to the actions of
a self-respecting, clear-visioned and upright man
when the position and arguments of that man are
unassailable is growing to be as typically American
as the manufacture of orange juice without oranges.
Only one Englishman has stooped to such a thing
in the last twenty-five years, and, for his pains, he
has since been a pariah among his fellows.

§ 4

Autobiography.—The common allegation that most autobiographies are in essence worthless because they are not honest may be true, but if it be true it is true for a reason that the critics do not, I believe, state with entire accuracy. In many cases, the autobiographer is entirely honest with himself. The fault lies rather in his inability to understand himself. He may honestly set forth what he believes to be the facts about himself, but those facts are not the true ones. It is a rare man, though he be as honest as the day is long, who knows himself. He may know himself in a general way, and even, in certain particulars, in an intimate way, but usually he is much of a stranger to himself. He may know how he reacts to the doctrines of Karl Marx, to a personable hussy and to camel's-hair underwear, but he has only a defective knowledge of his reactions to himself.

If all this seems a bit involved, let me be somewhat more explicit. Is there a man of even the most transcendent introspective gifts, of even the greatest clairvoyance so far as he himself is concerned, who knows why it is that he will periodically and involuntarily take a drink that he doesn't want, or be gracious to a person whom he dislikes, or buy a green tie that he knows in all likelihood he will never wear, or prolong a companionship •with a woman that inevitably and clearly promises trouble, or take physical risks that he plainly appreciates are senseless and dangerous, or strain his eyes reading at twilight when a mere slight move of the hand would turn on an electric switch, or eat fish in an Italian *table d'hôte,* or sit up half the night talking when he is so sleepy that he can hardly keep his eyes open? For every thing a man does rationally, he does another thing that, subsequently, he cannot for the life of him understand and intelligibly account for. Autobiography almost invariably presents only the man as he is able intelligibly and honestly to account for himself. This other phase of him, which may have colored his life far more greatly than he suspects, eludes him; not being able to comprehend it, he is unable to chronicle it. It is not that he is dishonest;

it is simply that he cannot see into the complex mystery, the jest of the gods, that he is.

§ 5

Book Reviewing in America.—With just four distinguished exceptions that I can think of, book reviewing on its more conspicuous levels in this country falls into a readily recognizable and perceptibly asinine technique. Among the leading reviewers of letters, aside from the quartette alluded to, it would seem to be a seldom violated tradition to approach a new book in the following manner:

1. An objection to any theme which disturbs the reviewer's personal philosophy in the matter of that theme.

2. A deploring of the fact that the author, instead of treating the present theme, did not treat of some other theme.

3. A cordial reception, regardless of the author's skill or lack of it, of any theme that finds a sympathetic response in the reviewer's psyche.

4. An objection to brilliance as brilliance save it be invested with emotion.

5. A deep-dyed conviction that, as between an Englishman and an American who write equally well, the Englishman is yet the better of the two.

6. A belief that all Germans over-write, and that their books might profitably be cut down by half.

7. A feeling that a young author, however ably he has done his job, is yet somehow lacking in something.

8. A conviction that humor is a smoke-screen designed to conceal lack of depth.

9. A hospitality to realism, yet a synchronous objection to vulgarity.

10. A belief that any book on Christ or Lincoln is a good book and any one on Swedenborg or Emma Goldman a bad one, and very funny.

§ 6

Melodrama.—It is a convention of criticism that melodrama, even at its best, is somehow peculiarly one of the dramatic sub-arts and that it must accordingly be treated with proper condescension. If this be true, the reason for its truth eludes me. The only way in which I can figure out the senseless prejudice is to recall the persistent custom of affixing definite labels to everything and, once they are duly affixed, of basing criticism upon the labels instead of upon what is in the bottles. The word *melodrama* has fallen into disrepute simply because the English critics, abandoning its exact meaning, began carelessly to employ it some forty-odd years ago to designate any play that they liked but felt they shouldn't like. Today, the word is never used with literal accuracy, but is used indiscriminately to describe any theatrical exhibit that doesn't fall with a ready click into one or another of the standard pigeon-holes. A drama in which a revolver is fired thus automatically becomes a melodrama. So does a genre study in which one of the characters steals money, is caught in the act by a policeman and avoids arrest by jumping out of the first-floor window and breaking the pane. So does a comedy that contains a safe hidden in the wall. So does a tragedy in which a railroad express train is even casually mentioned. The monkeyshines performed with the label are endless.

The detractors of melodrama—still using the word as it is currently employed—apparently never stop to think that their derogatory designation fits

many of the classics quite as closely as it fits the
modern plays upon which they slap it. If a melodrama is a play in which action is more important
than character, in which a character is influenced
from without rather than from within, and in which
emotions are played fortissimo, then "Electra" and
"Seven Before Thebes" are melodramas. If a melodrama is a play in which lust, murder, revenge
and physical action predominate, then "Macbeth"
and "Hamlet" are melodramas. If a melodrama is
a play in which a man bent upon evil disguises
himself, enters a house, commits a murder, is con-
fronted by a woman with an axe, jumps at her
with his bloody sword and, upon her running away
from him, chases her around until he catches up
with her and runs her through the gizzard, then the
"Choephoræ" of Æschylus is a melodrama. If a
melodrama is a play in which a woman of criminal
impulses meditates a Grand Guignol revenge and
slowly puts it into execution, then the "Medea" of
Euripides is a melodrama. And if a melodrama is
a play in which high emotion dominates and con-
trols rational thought, then the "Antigone" of

Sophocles is ten times the melodrama that "Sherlock Holmes" is.

§ 7

Jazz and Opera.—On the question of jazz rhythms applied to opera, objection has been raised by certain critical voices. It has been maintained that it is at once anachronistic and absurd to interpret the spirit of, say, the Louisiana of the 1830's in terms of relatively modern jazz. Such criticism is purely academic and technically imbecile. It might be argued analogously that it is at once equally anachronistic and absurd to interpret the spirit of the court of Herod 1830-odd years earlier in terms of Richard Strauss' Twentieth Century orchestral innovations. Criticism of this kind is worse than superficial; it gives a monkey-show at the expense of intelligence. The true objection to an association of jazz and opera goes considerably deeper. Jazz is a too cheap and shallow musical medium to evoke, convey and further any save cheap and shallow emotions. The passions of love and hate,

of exaltation and profound grief can no more be
interpreted by jazz than they can be interpreted by
a water-whistle. Jazz is an artificial musical stimu-
lant, designed primarily for dancers, boozers and
men with the emotional equipment of chorus girls.
It is to music what a ball-room floor is to the bed-
rock of the building itself. No more may an opera
—an opera in anything but name—be fashioned
out of it than a battle song may be made out of a
music-show moon tune.

§ 8

Study in Reviewing.—The reaction of four out
of every five American book reviewers to Sinclair
Lewis' admirable "Elmer Gantry" offers not only
meat to the student of native critical phenomena,
but a whole butcher-shop. It is the contention of
these reviewers that Lewis has made Gantry too
complete a charlatan and knave, that even in the
worst charlatan and knave there are streaks, albeit
often hidden, of the purest gold, and that the failure to indicate the latter in his central character
makes Lewis' novel an overly prejudiced and es-
sentially dubious job.

206

A FEW NOTES ON AMERICAN CRITICISM

A meditation of the reviewers' mental processes brings forth an idiosyncrasy of judgment that seems to me to be unmistakable. That judgment of Gantry is based, surely, not upon an appreciation and understanding of human beings as we unfortunately find them in this world, but rather upon human beings as we encounter them in literature. There was a time, and not so long ago as the clock ticks, when the scoundrels of popular literature were generally cut from a single slice of cloth—and very black it was—, when a hero was a hero and a villain was a villain, and when that was all there was to it. In those days, there were customarily, whether in novels or in plays, no shadings: a character was, so to speak, either a Rudolph Rassendyl or a Sir Francis Levison, either blond or brunet, either soft-shirted and hence a compendium of all the virtues, or clad in sinister evening clothes and hence a side-kick of the red boy. Rebellion against this order of things presently set in, and there followed a period, lasting until the present day, when it was arbitrarily demanded of practitioners of the art of letters and drama that they make their heroes less utterly heroic and their villains less utterly villainous. The old apothegm to the effect that there is some good in even the worst of us and some bad in even the best of us was lifted over bodily into the critical creed by all such reviewers as were wont to put faith in a wall-motto philosophy and who were given to a profound belief in the grandpa's-knee school of metaphysics, including as it did—in addition to the phylactery mentioned —such controvertible items as (*a*), it is always darkest just before dawn; (*b*), it never rains but it pours; and (*c*), an apple a day keeps the doctor away.

Following the injunction of these reviewers, susceptible authors began arbitrarily to leaven their characters. Heroes began to drink and swear, to have thoughts upon certain subjects that were not entirely noble, and even occasionally to forget their mothers' birthdays. And villains, in turn, began to drop pennies into blind beggars' cups on their way to bank robberies and, in the grand finale, just before the cops arrived on the scene, to hold out their hands to the heroines and assure them contritely that if ever in the future they needed help they, the villains, would be waiting out there in the West to come to them. It was all less honest and deeply plumbed human nature than superficial literary and theatrical hocus-pocus, designed cheaply to capture the sympathetic attention of the authors' customers, and of a piece with the cunning of so many highwaymen who politely inquire the time of day of a pedestrian before black-jacking him and stealing his watch. For one author who understood the mystery of human nature and was able beautifully to get its deviousness onto paper, there were a hundred who understood it not at all, but who simply faked it and tried to get reality and persuasion into their characters by following the demanded chameleon ritual and parroting feebly at a distance the comprehension of their superiors. For one author who anatomized human nature shrewdly and truthfully, there were many more who merely substituted what may be called literary and theatrical human nature and who contrived not characters that would be recognized as real by their Maker so much as characters who would be accepted as real by a herd of dolts, whose minds followed horse-car tracks.

As I have said, this attitude persists to the present day. The reviewers, their minds saturated with fiction, remain thoroughly convinced that a man who murders his family, burns down the house and then goes into the back-yard and sabres his grandmother is nevertheless a virtuoso of "Onward, Christian Soldiers" on the accordion and unquestionably recites the Sixth Commandment to himself a dozen or more times every night at bedtime. True to the modern copy-book view of mortals, they remain positive that, over a definite and given point of time, no man may be absolutely good or absolutely bad, as Uncle Tom was or as Simon Legree was. The Uncle Toms of present-day literature must, in their sapient contemplation of the world, have elements of Legree, and the Legrees elements of Uncle Tom. They believe that Jack-the-Ripper used the paper-knife with which he opened his worshipped mother's daily letters, and that Dr. Crippen was at moments indistinguishable from the Rollo boys.

§ 9

Comedy and Drama.—The theory that there is something a bit recreant and even imputable about comedy still casts its shadow over much of American critical writing. Nail down the native critic as to which, given his choice, he would write a leading essay about for the *Yale Review*—Brieux's "Maternité" or Brieux's "Les Hannetons" —and he will pick the former without fail. Or at least some drama as opposed to some comedy, however superior the latter may actually be. There is that about comedy that seems relatively petty to him; he cannot persuade himself to believe that, even at its best, it is quite so important as what he calls drama. What men laugh at—even very intelligent men—he imagines cannot be so worthy of his attention as what men—even sentimental and lack-wit men—cry over. A serious dramatist, in his eyes, is one who treats gravely a theme that a really more profound dramatist might treat lightly. The attitude takes him to even greater and more donkeyish lengths. When a Hauptmann turns from a "Weavers" to a "Beaver Coat" or a Björnson from a "Beyond Human Power" to a "Geography and Love," he cannot rid himself of the impression that the dramatist is merely taking a fling, a day off from seriousness, and is hence for the nonce to be treated with a degree of condescension. He declines to accept the dramatist's wisdom of temporarily altered point of view, made necessary and desirable by the nature of his materials, and opposes him with the ignorance of his persistent and inflexible point of view.

In comedy, as such a critic would appreciate were he to trouble to investigate, we find most of the true, deep, biting intelligence that has come down to us throughout the history of the drama. Comedy has made the human race wise, where drama has made it but merciful. It is comedy that has purged men of their delusions, where drama has only furthered and supported the latter. Aristophanes made his fellow-countrymen salubriously cognizant of their affectations, shams and hypocrisies; so Molière made his; so Shaw makes his today. The Greeks profited vastly more from the purgative humor of their comic writers than from the blood and agony of their tragic. It would take a highly imaginative historian, and one gifted in the art of sleight-of-hand, to convince any of us that actual Greek civilization was not benefited immensely more by "Lysistrata," the "Clouds," the "Wasps," the "Frogs," "Peace" and similar exhibits than by all the mock Orestes, Electras, Agamemnons and Clytemnestras who strutted its stages. It was Shakespeare's lofty verse that made men dream dreams, but it was his comic wit and irony that made them undream them to their own greater advantage.

§ 10

Censorship.—Literary and dramatic censorship rests largely upon the assumption that dirty words are conductive to a corruption of morals. Dirty words never corrupted the morals of anyone, young or old. If morals are corrupted at all, they are corrupted by dirty ideas cleanly and hence attractively and romantically expressed. The most aphrodisiacal book written since the Year of Our Lord 1800 hasn't a single word in it that the censors might object to. The least aphrodisiacal book written since the same year, a book that wouldn't cause an emotional flurry in even a fashionable girls' finishing-school, is full of words that would make a longshoreman blush. Our friend Satan knows his business. He writes English as immaculate and as shrewdly suggestive as a virgin picking daisies while enemy troops are marching by.

THE GASTRONOMIC CAPITAL

From the dark sinfulness of the city of New York at least one beam of light shoots up and bathes the heavens in its pure glow, one beam that beckons the traveler and guides his footsteps toward an unmistakable reward. Corned beef and cabbage eaters from the rock-ribbed coasts of New England, hogmeat chewers from the prairie States, Chilibean gorgers from the southlands, rump gobblers from the West—all soon or late see the light from a distance and, means permitting, make to follow it. For in New York, for all its lack of other godly virtues, they, together with the rest of the modern world, have come to find the gastronomic capital of the nation and not only of the nation but, very probably, of countries far and wide.

There was a time, and not more than fifteen years ago, when eating in New York, with negligible exception, was about on a par with eating at a Holland railway junction. Aside from a relatively few tables like Delmonico's, Sherry's, Lüchow's and the Petit Vefour of blessed memory, the general run of food was more or less stereotyped and hardly of the sort to make men's conversation water. But since the war has come and gone, the city has made strides so remarkable in the direction of fine eating that today it stands without a serious rival. For one first-class cuisine in London like the Tour Eiffel or Boulesin's or the Savoy Grill, New York boasts fifty; and for one in Paris like the Montagné, Larue's, Madame Gélot's or Foyot's, it is a simple matter to find a double number in New York quite as good if not actually much superior. Travel the world over today and you will find no food better prepared or more various or more toothsome than you will find in New York at the Colony, or at Robert's, or at Billy the Oyster Man's, or at the Polignac, or at the Cyrano, or at Del Pezzo's, or at the humble Dinty Moore's, or at a hundred and one other places, big and little, expensive and cheap, American, German, Italian, Swedish, French, Slavic and what not.

The question naturally occurs at this point as to how this dispensation has happened to come about.

216

The answer is to be found, first, in the consequences of the late struggle to make the world safe
for the banking interests. The end of the war, one
need hardly go to the trouble of pointing out at
this late hour, left the residents in the fighting countries in hard straits and among these residents not
the least were those gentlemen whose profession
and art lay in the preparation of dishes for the
palates of connoisseurs. Connoisseurs and plenty
there were, but unfortunately the war left nothing
in their pockets longer to connoisseur with. The
hundreds, even thousands, of talented oven-profes-
sors and chefs thus found themselves without any
outlet for their virtuosity and, what was worse, no
other means wherewith to earn a livelihood. What
to do? Well, there was just one thing to do and that
was to get together enough money to buy a ticket
to America and set up shop there. And so it came
about that presently there were in gala activity in
New York fully three-quarters of the best cooks
and kitchen *tonadilleros* of France, Germany, Italy,
Austria, Russia and Belgium, to say nothing of
countries somewhat less renowned among the gour-
mets. I do not use the "three-quarters" idly. It is

an established fact that in New York at the moment you will find fifteen of the eighteen most competent stove-presiders of pre-war Paris, no less than three dozen German kitchen eminentos, all save two, I am informed by expert statisticians, of the flower of pre-war Italian cuisines and, if your taste runs that way, about every Russian of high food purveying gifts save perhaps the personal and private dish-confector to the late lamented Tsar. And there are some who say that even he is to be discovered in the person of the gentleman who officiates over the oven of a Russian eating-house in the West Fifties.

To New York, in mass formation, these gifted European fellows have brought all their long and memorable skill in the concoction of edibles for the fascination and enchantment of the palate of *Homo Americanus.* The money is here to pay them well; the customers are here in infinite number to crowd their places of business; the variously inclined tastes of all the different bloods that flow in the American melting pot offer the proper challenge to their devious and endless repertoire. Nor are these foreign professors in absolute control of the scene. Their coming has challenged, in turn, the best that was in the home team, so to speak, and the latter, nobly facing the hot competition, have exerted themselves to the utmost to keep pace with the demands of the trade. The result has been not only a very considerable improvement in the quality of even hotel food—before the war, save in two or three cases, pretty terrible—but also in the quality of food served in the cheaper, standardized restaurants. In the instance of the latter, three specific chains of restaurants today serve food, at very reasonable prices, that is actually twice as good as that which one got before the war at certain of the tony, exclusive and expensive cafés.

I do not wish to intimate that New York has a monopoly of all the good eating-places in America. In many of the larger cities, and in certain of the smaller ones, you will be able to discover a place or two where the table is certainly no mean shakes. For example, Antoine's in New Orleans and the Victor Hugo in Los Angeles. But New York remains the capital. There you will find the best that every nation in the world has to offer in the way of food; there you will find a variety that cannot be matched in any other city in Christendom; there you will find a multiplicity of restaurants that, for the quality of food, the preparation of food and the service of food, are the wonder of present-day civilization. Do you crave French cooking in the grand manner? Then you will find nothing in all France—and I am sufficiently conscious of the superlative, as is my Little Mary—so consistently excellent as that which you will find at the Colony restaurant in the East Sixties. Do you long for Italian cooking of the sort to make Mussolini himself loosen his belt? Then try the delicacies at Moneta's down in Mulberry Street. Or perchance your fancy runs to a discreet combination of the two schools? Then I give you the cuisine of the estimable M. Bergonzi in the West Forties. Say that it is the Russian technique that entertains you. I point out, then, the Samarkand in the East Fifties. Or mayhap the German. My finger directs you to the Kloster Glocke in lower Fourth Avenue. Or, very likely, it is something Japanese. Then you will travel far in Japan itself to beat what you will get at the Miyako in the West Fifties. As for Turkish delights, the Sultan's own august tonsils would moisten were he to sit down to table in the West Thirties, and as for American, let the band strike up "The Star Spangled Banner" for the Castle Cave, where there are beef-steaks what are beef-steaks, and such potatoes cooked in bacon as Stonewall Jackson himself never knew, and such baked oysters as would make the Governor of Maryland leave home without waiting to put on his hat. The mere Governor of Maryland? I state the case too mildly. Let me make it the whole staff of the Rennert Hotel in Baltimore, that erstwhile *Kaiserstadt* of oysterdom.

Fifteen years ago, as I have observed, the signal medallists of the cook-oven, the beys and satraps of the culinary art, were to be found in three or four isolated kitchens. Twenty and twenty-five years ago, they were confined to perhaps not more than two metropolitan kitchens. Thirty and forty years ago, a single one was monarch of all he surveyed. The so-called mauve decade pretty well exhausted its boast when it called off the names of Oscar, Sherry, Delmonico and Martin. But the celebrated progeneration of rabbits is as naught compared with the metaphorical offspring of these venerables of yesterday. Where there was one chef of rank, there are now twenty. No longer is it only the affluent man who can dine well in New York; the man of moderate means can today get himself such meals as his father and grandfather would have sat down and composed books about. We hear of the wonderful dinner one used to be able to get in New York for a dollar. True enough, it is no longer to be had for a dollar—for the dollar isn't what it used to be—but it is to be had for *two* dollars. And two dollars, as the change has come about in money, may hardly be put down as only a rich man's price.

To enumerate the places in New York where one may experience the joys of the middle in a veritably yohimbin manner would be to present a catalogue, while not quite of a Sears-Roebuck bulk, yet size-able enough. I have engaged the hundred and one curries of the Orient, but never have I found any so perfectly prepared as those at the Ceylon-India restaurant in the West Forties, where, in the midst of one's enravishment, one may at any moment find a migratory cockatoo roosting placidly on one's shoulder. I have eaten my way for hours through smörgasbord after smörgasbord in the Scandinavian countries (preparing myself for the night's tussle with Ibsen, Björnson and Strindberg), but none has offered so stupendous a repertoire as the one that will dismay you at Henry's in the West Thirties. General Robert E. Lee himself, I venture, never tasted such fried chicken, sweet potato pie and waffles as any present-day rear private may gorge himself with at no less than three different restaurants in Harlem known to the first policeman you happen to meet at any street corner north of 125th Street. I have eaten my way up and down the Paris boulevards and the Leipzigerstrasse and Unter den Linden and all around the Kärntner-ring and the length of Piccadilly, and if there is a single eating establishment on any one of them or near any one of them that can match Henri's over the Lynnbrook road or the Hofbräu over the Hoboken ferry I must have missed it. I shall not bore you with further statistics, though I should like to mention in passing that if you have ever waxed enthusiastic over the *hors d'œuvre* at the Coq d'Or in Paris, I wish you'd see how you react to those at the Mirliton, and if you've ever grown unduly excited over the meats at Simpson's in London (even in the good old days), I urge you to see what your mouth says when those at the Three Star Chop House or Professor Moore's enter it. Then, by way of comparing notes further, I might suggest that, before you dismiss this general encomium as a bit too extravagant, you jump into a taxi and take a whirl at the Mexican dishes at Fornos', the Oriental dainties (one's lips dampen at the memory of them!) at the pride of East Nineteenth Street, the salads at the Maison Arthur, the endless variety of sea food at the Oyster Bay, the pressed duck at the Madison, the tier upon tier of pasties at Voisin's, the Bavarian masterpieces at Lüchow's, the frogs' legs at Ben Reilly's, the lobster in any one of a dozen forms at White's, the—but I promised I would refrain from cataloguing.

In the midst of all this eloquence, I hear, however, a protesting voice from the thitherward cities. Restaurants, restaurants, restaurants! it cries, not without a trace of sniffishness. What about the best of all cooking, to wit, home cooking? Of that, at its best, you will find none in New York! But won't you, my hearties? While I do not profess to be an authority on home cooking as it obtains in every part of the United States—after all, a man can travel only so much and eat only eight or ten regular meals a day—, I venture the humble opinion that if so-called home cooking is any better in Pittsburgh, St. Louis, San Francisco or Wanz Falls, Dakota, than I have found it to be in New York, it must be pretty doggone good. Against the cooking in any home this side of Coronado Beach, I stand ready to offer my undershirt at odds of two to one on that on exhibition at the ménage of Robert H. Davis, known to the world of letters as Bob, or of Olof H. Lamm, the eminent consul, or of Fred Muschenheim, who owns the Hotel Astor and who lives around the corner from it, or of my compatriot, the M. Hermann Oelrichs, or of any one of a dozen others whose names I shall be glad to send in a plain wrapper on receipt of two cents in stamps. If home cooking ever reached the heights that it reaches at tables like these, H. G. Wells' "Outline of History" has left out something. Davis' dinners, with three dozen oysters and a pint of cocktail sauce serving as a prologue to a procession of tureens steaming with such viands as no mother ever had the faintest idea how to cook, with a roast beef the size of the Louvre and potatoes piled as high as cannon balls at Waterloo and pies as large as Falstaff's waistline, to say nothing of cheeses big enough to make a Dutch housewife open her mouth in awe—Davis' dinners must be seen, to say nothing of attacked, to be even vaguely appreciated. And as for those contrived by the engaging Muschenheim at his private board (not to be confused with his hotel), they need no celebration by me. Sinclair Lewis, Theodore Dreiser, Ernest Boyd, Roda-Roda, Arthur Bodanzky, Toscanini, these and many others have already sung their praises in public conversation, in music, and in print. I have said that I stand ready to offer my chemise at odds of two to one that home cooking has nowhere excelled that on tap at this Muschenheim table. I now increase the odds to ten to one, and throw in my suspenders handsomely embroidered with American eagles. I hope I betray no secret when I tell you that at one dinner at this extraordinary table (and it was just an ordinary, every-night dinner, not a special one), the author of "Main Street" and "Babbitt" and "Elmer Gantry" found the remarkable cooking so irresistible that he ate ten helpings of baby lamb and roast potatoes, thus falling behind, by three helpings, the author of "Sister Carrie," "Jennie Gerhardt" and "An American Tragedy." As for your humble servant, he reports with shame that he was unable to cope with such masters of the literary art, the best that he could do being nine helpings, not counting four plates of soup, three helpings of filet of sole, six prune tarts and maybe thirty or forty hot biscuits.

To return briefly and by way of coda to our initial motif. The day when the secrets of the culinary art were in the keeping of four or five outstanding and high-priced chefs in New York is definitely passed. To the mysteries of that art countless newcomers have become privy, and trick upon trick has been further added to the store of magic by the professors who have come to us from overseas. As a consequence, there is such a gastronomic show on view in New York today as must satisfy the demands of even the most finicky customer. I conclude with a very simple but relevant and perhaps significant remark. Ten years ago, there were just two places in New York where you might get beef tastefully prepared in any one of three ways. To-day, you can get it tastefully prepared in no less than sixty, and in any one of twenty ways.

SHOW-CASE SAMPLES

§ 1

The Emperor.—Much of the fault that is found by
Americans with the Hon. Calvin Coolidge as President of their country undoubtedly rests, at bottom,
upon the unromantic aspect of the fellow. 'Way
down below the groans and grunts uttered over
him, 'way down below the ostensible reasons for
the dissatisfaction with him, runs the inevitable current of popular distaste for a leader who lacks
picturesqueness. In the way of romance and pic-
turesque quality, Coolidge cuts a sorry figure. He
lacks even Harding's impressive front or Taft's
sizeable bulk, warm geniality and English actor-
manager *Schnurrbart*. When his likeness is flashed
on a movie sheet, it is, indeed, always necessary
carefully to identify him on the screen by name
that the audience may not mistake him for a casual
delegate to some School Teachers' Convention,
Bible Congress or other such news-reel excitement

and may be induced to bestow upon him the usual perfunctory handclaps.

That the Hon. Calvin is himself privy to this embarrassing deficiency on his part is obvious. And equally transparent are the means he adopts in an effort to remedy it, or at least to conceal it in so far as possible. The periodic pilgrimages to the little old New England home town with the ritualistic democratic shaking of hands with the town plumber and barber; the Sunday morning visit to the little frame country church with the small boys of the village trailing behind in the same impressed manner with which they are wont to follow the blonde bareback rider in the Walter L. Main circus parade; the histrionic tightened lips and scholarly frown customarily associated in the public mind with great statesmen; the slouchy clothes associated in the same mind with genius—these devices the Hon. Calvin utilizes to assist him in throwing the hero-worshippers off the scent. But to small end. For here is the first President that the United States has had since Lincoln who doesn't possess a single quality to gratify the fancy and imagination of his people, who hasn't a single characteristic—save taciturnity, which is a sedative to the public's imagination rather than a stimulating bolus—to distinguish him from the common run of male mammals. He is, in point of fact, the only President in the last sixty years whom stage comedians cannot give impersonations of, since there is absolutely nothing about him that differentiates him from the ordinary man: whether in habit, manner, dress, look or speech. He hasn't even so much as Grant's cigar, Hayes' beer-brewer's watch-fob, Cleveland's fishing-pole, McKinley's Roman nose, Roosevelt's sombrero or Woodrow's campus elegance to stamp him apart from a million other men. And so his subjects feel that something is wrong with him and show their disapproval by finding fault with him in directions where he actually is not at fault. The leader of a nation may be a dolt and a doodle, but so long as there is something romantic about him his people will venerate him. But if he have not about him a certain magic of personality, a certain striking theatricality, his people will soon or late hoot him, though he possess the wisdom of a Frederick the First and the genius of a Frederick the Second.

§ 2

In Memoriam.—The late William Jennings Bryan goes down into history as the shrewdest and most adept self-advertiser that America has known. The fellow's genius in this respect was awe-inspiring. The moment one publicity dodge showed signs of petering out, he was ready with another and even better one. Politics, war, theology, science—each provided meat for his sandwich. Even his death was calculated with an eye to the main chance. If he had died on a week-day, he would have got a column on the first pages of the newspapers and the rest of the story would have been buried on the inside. So, astutely aware that Sunday is the dullest news day of the week and that the Monday papers are always hard up for news, he cleverly passed out on the Sabbath, with the result that half of the first pages throughout the country were his.

§ 3

A Forgotten Man.—With monuments being erected monthly all over the land to such members of the nation's illustrious deceased as second-rate New

England poets, Civil War profiteers, medicine-men of the Ojibway tribe, presidents of tank-town colleges, founders of orphan asylums and builders of the Gowanus Canal, I put in a demand that one man who has been completely overlooked by the memento professors be honored at once with a tasty statue, monument, obelisk or horse-hitching post. I allude to the late Hon. Charles C. Hall, inventor of the modern collar-button, a man who did more for his fellow Americans than all the statues that ever stuck hands into Prince Alberts or pointed prognosticating fingers at amatory couples on park benches. Among the services rendered by Americans to their countrymen, none is more important than that rendered by Hall. To say against his service that it was an obvious one and one that must have been rendered at one time or another by some other man if Hall hadn't got there first, is as foolish as to argue that if Balboa hadn't discovered the Pacific Ocean, Hiram Johnson would have in due time. Hall made the egg stand, and to Hall goes the credit.

Yet Hall, like many another such man, is neglected and memorials are erected instead to individ-

uals who deserve them much less than he does.
A rich marble shaft is put up in honor of a dog
whose barking saved the lives of two osteopaths,
three Elks and a corset manufacturer when a house
burned down, and the man who invented and gave
the lead pencil to the world is allowed to rot forgotten in his grave. Monuments are raised in honor
of William Cullen Bryant, Horace Mann, Maria
Mitchell, Oscar S. Straus and Pawnee Bill, and the
memory of the men who gave America the Pullman club-car, the steam radiator, the curved tooth-
brush, the coat-shirt, the Boston garter, Michelob
beer, open plumbing, the modern envelope and
Pond's Extract is left to the worms.

§ 4

An Ambassador.—Of all the men whom the Republic has sent as ambassadors to the courts of
Europe, none, I believe, has been so authentic and
representative an American as the Hon. Alexander
Pollock Moore, late head of the *corps diplomatique*
in Madrid. The usual American minister pleni-
potentiary is less an American than an imitation
Englishman: a fellow who has cultivated a polit-

ical bedside manner and a social suavity to the point where he can use the broad *a* without feeling too self-conscious and where he can wear a silk hat without getting a headache. The courts of Europe have long been full of such pseudo-Americans who no more fool the nations they are assigned to than a Bull Durham sign fools a cow. The spectacle of one of these *de luxe* hicks in silk knickers, spouting French and trying to look like Arthur Balfour is enough to send the other ambassadors to the pantry to stifle their horse-laughs. The estimable Moore of Pittsburgh, Pa., was, on the other hand, a bird of different feather. A Knight Templar, a Mystic Shriner, an Elk, and the Lord knows what else, he was as thoroughly and incontrovertibly American as One-Eyed Connolly and baked beans. He was the only representative of the United States abroad in the last fifteen years who was content to present himself personally for what he actually was—a plain, everyday, jolly super-Rotarian—and who didn't bother to be any more British in speech, manner and conduct than the *Oberkellner* of a Munich beerhouse. Where the average American ambassador, when he gives a

reception, seeks to make an impression on the
capital he is accredited to by filling the em-
bassy with visiting American moneybags, corn-belt
mayors and social pushers, Moore filled the dump
with vaudeville hoofers, pretty "Follies" girls,
baseball players, prize-fighters and jazz band
leaders—in short, with precisely the kind of Americans the Spaniards were most greatly interested
in, and so endeared himself to the latter where
the other ambassadors have bored everyone to
death. Moore, to the Spaniards, was the archetype
of American, as, indeed, he must have been to
every other European nation. The other nuncios
are, the most of them, simply preposterous actors,
half-British, half-American, with their monocles
constantly getting out of place, with their spats
half a size too large for them, with their French
the French of Ritz bus-boys, and with their polish
the polish of so many stock company Jenkinses and
Pottses. More representatives like Moore would
earn for us the respect that we currently do not
get from Europe, since his naturalness, lack of
affectation and personal honesty would evoke the
esteem that the current omnipresent headwaiter

diplomats fail to. A Mystic Shriner, an Elk and an admirer of soft-shoe dancers may not, perhaps, constitute the ideal American ambassador, but he surely constitutes a vastly better and a vastly more engaging one than a Berlitz sophomore in a Truly Warner silk hat who has laboriously coached himself how to bow like the late Charles Hawtrey.

§ 5

Mr. Bok's Contribution to Science.—Edward W. Bok has made numerous contributions toward the improvement of the native scene. It was largely through his editorship of the *Ladies' Home Journal* that an increased respect for interior decoration that wasn't an eye-sore was initially inculcated in at least a portion of the great American yokelry. It was through the same journal that women in the smaller American towns were initially brought to embellish their bodies in a manner that would no longer scare the cows eating grass along the street-car tracks. It was Bok who created the $100,000 American Peace Award and who published "The Young Man in Business," "The Americanization of Edward Bok," and other such inspirations to the young American. But in none of these has the estimable Philadelphian so proved his sagacity and so contributed to the psychical or physical beauty of his fellow Americans as he has in another and hitherto unannounced direction.

I hope I betray no secret when I divulge Mr. Bok's discovery and practice, which, once they are known, will doubtless promptly be followed by every male who has any sense left. It is Mr. Bok's invariable rule to have his tailor measure him for his suits not standing up, as has been the custom from time immemorial—a custom that has produced the worst-dressed lot of male human beings in Christendom—but, on the contrary, *sitting down*. Mr. Bok has figured, and rightly, that for one minute the average man is on his feet he is half an hour seated, and that, accordingly, when his clothes are fitted to him in an upright position, he looks pretty much a dud when he is sitting, which is most of the time. The result of the M. Bok's sartorial cogitations has made him appear to be the best dressed and most accurately tailored man in America, at least for a relatively greater daily period than any of his fellows. For a man to have a suit prepared for him from measurements made while he is standing is as ridiculous as to have a hat tried on him while he is lying down. It has remained for the Mons. Bok to make this fact known, and prosperously, to his dunderheaded brothers. Now that they are privy to it, they need no longer be embarrassed because of an unwitting display of sock-garters every time they seat themselves and cross their legs, or be made uncomfortable and unsightly by a coat collar that crawls up to their ears, by sleeves that pull half way up their forearms, by trousers that strain mercilessly at the nether anatomy, and by waistcoats that slide three-quarters of the way up the abdomen.

§ 6

E. W. Howe.—Some years ago, in younger and less careworn days, Mencken and I magnanimously offered ourselves to the American people as candidates for the offices of President and Vice-President of the United States—which office either of us would be chosen for, we didn't care; we would shoot dice to settle the matter after election. We announced our platform, which contained not only one hundred things we would do if elected but a considerable number of others that we promised on our oaths not to do. One of the first things we stipulated we would do would be to select E. W. Howe, of Kansas, as our Secretary of State.

I betray no secret when I say that we were neither nominated nor elected, since the opacity of the American public is sufficiently recognized by this time. Instead of being treated seriously, our offer to come to our country in the hour of its need, and sacrifice four years—eight, if necessary—of our lives, our experience and our wisdom to its service was dismissed lightly, even, I am grieved to report, in certain quarters with a share of unseemly humor. But out of our defeat, one lingering impression emerges. Out of a prank there stands and remains, blinking in the light, at least one sliver of good, hard, common sense. The circumstance that it was vested in the floppy pantaloons of satirical burlesque does not entirely conceal it. And what, to repeat, is this sliver of common sense? It is that Mr. E. W. Howe, of Kansas, would actually make a first-rate Secretary of State and would so raise the percentage of that cabinet post, which currently resembles the batting average of the 1898 Louisville baseball team, at least ninety per cent.

Ed Howe, as he is familiarly known to all persons with whom he is not familiar, is one of the clearest thinking, unbuncombed, unsentimental, practical men in this country still out of the Atlanta Penitentiary. He has his share of peculiar cerebrations, to be sure. He believes and stoutly maintains, for example, that Henry Ford is a greater man than Michelangelo and that John D. Rockefeller is a greater one than Brahms. He believes that there is automatically more virtue in a man who lives on a cow pasture than in one who lives on Park Avenue. He believes that all critics should be gagged and bound and thrown into the nearest available sewer, thus, at one swoop, inferentially ridding the world for all time of such nuisances as Huxley, Voltaire and Jesus Christ. He believes that money-making is one of the noblest aims of the human being, and that the man who prefers the painting of pictures or the writing of books or the composing of a symphony to starting a chain of grocery stores is a plain damned fool, and to be greatly pitied. He believes that Atchison, Kansas, is a better place to live in than New York, and—say what you will against him—heroically practises what he preaches. But for every such bizarre philosophy he has a dozen that are not only practical, sober and sound but that, in an age of drooling balderdash, sweep over this yesman's-land like a sweet breeze.

Readers of Howe's *Monthly* and of his various books have long observed in the fellow a brand of clear vision on national affairs shared by few of his countrymen. The prevalent, popular buncombe makes no more impression upon him than common sense makes upon the political mountebanks at Washington. The late war, together with its hypocrisies, flag-waggings and solemn rodomontade, drew only a sardonic guffaw from him: he was one of the very few Americans—and certainly no member of Dr. Brander Matthews' National Institute of Arts and Letters can accuse him of being a hyphenate—who spoke the truth about the war when to speak the truth called for a high virtuosity in dodging spittoons. The ignominious gullibility of the British toe-kissers, the hysterical

Lafayette-worshippers who view France in the light of a "Pope's nose" and constitute themselves Richmond Pearson Hobsons on all occasions, the patriotic charlatans who still speak of all Union Hill, New Jersey, bartenders as Huns, the whole kit and caboodle of Washington frauds and fakers he sees through at a glance and plants his boot dexterously where it will do the most good. Though he lives in a God-forsaken little dump in a God-forsaken part of a God-forsaken land, his spirit is infinitely cosmopolitan and his heart has in it the understanding and wisdom of a man revolving within the very hub of life. He likes to dub himself a yokel; that is one of his foolish little vanities. He is anything but a yokel. He is a citizen of the world.

He is, as I have hinted, almost completely anæsthetic to fine art. As a critic of art he is so bad, indeed, that he would make an excellent and highly admired writer for any metropolitan daily newspaper. The more sensitive of his readers bawl and squirm every time a copy of his *Monthly* is delivered at their doors. But one cannot expect too much of a man otherwise so well equipped for high office in a democratic state. Also, he is given to estimating beauty in terms of morality. If an artist has been guilty of moral *faux pas*, Howe simply denies that the fellow is an artist and lets it go at that. One cannot look to him for opinions in such departments. But if one wants intelligence in other matters, if one wants unemotional thinking on the various ramifications of the national life, his is the table to sit at. The church, business, politics, marriage, the home, local government—on such topics you will find him dispensing well-rounded pearls. For the readily assimilable stencils he has no use. He doesn't care where the chips fly; if some of them hit himself, all the better. He is a searching critic of his country and its people because, first and foremost, he is a searching critic of himself as an American.

I have met him only once—and then very briefly. Some years ago, on one of his visits to New York, Mencken and I called on him at his hotel and spent perhaps half an hour with him. He sat, I recall, on the edge of his bed and confined himself—after the first formalities were over—to telling us of a wonderful vaudeville show he had seen the night before at the Hippodrome. What Mencken and I talked about, I don't remember: doubtless the transient nothings usual to brief and casual first meetings. But Howe left his mark on my memory none the less. Some men can talk brilliantly to you for an hour and still leave little impression remaining after a week has passed. Others can say nothing, and yet you remember them for years. Howe is such a one. You feel about him that, beneath that simple and innocent exterior of his, there is something as deep-running as the waters. He has charm, a very great charm. He has simplicity, and where a more valuable quality? He has wisdom, though he leaves it to you to find out. He has tolerance and breadth and a devil's eye to sham and pretense. Not to know him from his writings is not to know one of the most thoroughly worthwhile of living Americans.

DELUSIONS

§ 1

The American Distrust of Wit.—It is a distinguishing characteristic of the American that he distrusts wit as he distrusts a female 'cello player or a too jovial physician. Instead of discerning in and behind it a mind that, having mastered all the platitudes and grown properly skeptical of most of them, indulges itself in a searching and prophylactic criticism in terms of irony, he appraises wit as being merely the refuge of a none too profound intelligence and its entrepreneur, at best, as something of a clown. Thus, there is no surer pitfall for the aspirant to popular esteem than that of polished humor, as many a hopeful public character has learned only too late. A certain amount of obvious and harmless jocosity is privileged such a man, but, even so, very sparingly and then only if it be of a safe, drugstore almanac quality.

This suspicion of wit is ever peculiar to democ-

246

racies, though in the United States it has attained to a degree not hitherto matched. It is an outstanding mark of the democratic man that he puts trust in and believes not serious and profound ideas but rather hollow and superficial ideas seriously and profoundly expressed. It is not the content but the manner of articulation that wooes and fetches him. This is a secret sufficiently known, of course, to professors of the public emotion, and by its sedulous exercise they profit and prevail in the democratic community. It is as impossible to imagine the flourishing of a Disraeli in a democracy as it is to imagine a democracy without a Walter Hines Page.

§ 2

Democracy.—The failure of democracy is of a piece with the failure of marriage since the so-called emancipation of women. Where there is the theory of equality among persons living under the same roof or under the same flag there can be no sound and workable organization. National content, permanent prosperity, happiness and strength in unity are to be obtained only where there is an outstanding dictator, and such a dictator, like the successful husband, must be born not out of the hypothetically shrewd meditation of his people or, in the instance of the husband, of his wife, but out of their romance and willing subservience. A king was the father of Cinderella's prince. Men may follow, but they do not and never will lay down their lives, their intelligence and their derisory humor for a fellow citizen from a cow State in a Stein-Bloch three-piece suit, an Arrow collar and a Dunlap derby hat.

§ 3

The Holy Howlers.—The denunciation of the sensational methods of those auctioneers of God who perform in our Sunday pulpits leaves me, upon meditation, a bit cold. Religion is not successfully to be inculcated in the sheep in any other manner, nor has it ever been. If the Rev. Dr. Isadore Tongueberg today preaches the Word in terms of tabloid newspaper headlines, let us remember that Moses did likewise. If the Rev. Dr. Ferdinand Gabjaw today preaches Christ in the manner of a vaudeville magician, let us not overlook the fact

248

that Matthew, Mark, Luke and John preceded him in the technique. And before we heave a soft pie at Billy Sunday, let us think of the Wesley brothers.

§ 4

The Next War.—There have recently appeared several tomes dealing more or less profoundly with the possible origin of the next war. Like the tomes that in turn preceded them, they present us with the spectacle of so many doctors of military science, economics, world politics and sociology sacrificing themselves to severe headaches in a brave effort to make study and investigation in their several arts dovetail persuasively with the next gala discharge of cannon. I have a feeling that the arduous labors to which these estimable gentlemen are devoting themselves are largely useless. Just as the last war was started simply by a bad boy in the European flea belt with a loose pistol, so will the next one doubtless be started by something equally unforeseen, unanalyzable and relatively insignificant. Let a hitherto impeccable Jap bartender far gone in rice wine hit an American sailor over the head with a bungstarter, let a French rear private off on leave and coming down the steps of the peep-show at No. 28 Rue Brey bump into and knock down a British lieutenant-colonel going up them, or let a German pretzel-baker sing "Die Wacht am Rhein" too loudly in Lorraine on the fourteenth of July, and the fun will probably start all over again.

§ 5

Philosophy.—E. W. Howe wrote not long ago, "A philosophy requiring a large volume is too much; a hundred pages is enough." Cut the number of pages down to seventy-five, and one comes closer to the truth. There is no philosophy, however profound, that can't clearly be expressed in relatively few words; the rest are mere decoration and embellishment which betray even the greatest philosopher's disturbing qualifications and doubts or perhaps his mere desire to impress by size and weight. The bigger the book, the smaller the philosopher's self-assurance and self-conviction.

250

§ 6

Experience.—In the common acceptance of the term, a man's experience, for a reason I can't quite make out, is generally associated in the popular mind with trouble. Thus, when we hear that a man has profited by experience, we are asked to believe that his experience has consisted in trials and tribulations. Yet the experience from which a man profits most is vastly less that which has been related to his miseries and woes than that which has been related to his successes and happiness. A man learns little from his defeats; it is his triumphs—in business, in poker, in artistic effort, or in amour—that give him his most valuable tips and teach him his most valuable lessons.

§ 7

The After-Life.—The doctrine of the after-life, as expounded by the rev. clergy, is based upon the optimistic theory that if the cook drops a cheap china soup-plate, breaks it into a hundred pieces and lets them lie on the floor long enough, they

necktie, vest and lap are covered with mementoes of his virtuosity. It is thus that one can tell the exercising American a block off. That is, the one who has passed his thirtieth year and still keeps up the nonsense. In order to revive himself after the immediate and superficial stimulation of his physical monkeyshines has worn off, he is driven to keep himself going with alcohol. Such local expressions as "the nineteenth hole," "the tenth inning," "65-love" and "a Johnny Walker massage" are illuminating.

The effect of exercise on professionals or on persons who devote their careers to it—and who are physically best fitted to indulge in it—should be closely regarded by persons, not so well equipped, who engage in it, as the curious phrase has it, for pleasure. If there is, with the single exception of Miss Helen Wills, a woman tennis player or swimmer or horse fanatic or gutta-percha ball pounder who, even in her late twenties, doesn't look like an old apple, I am either taking the wrong rotogravure section or losing my eyesight. With the single exception of James J. Corbett, who can think of a prize-fighter who, at forty-five, hasn't been viewed by Frank Campbell with gleeful, appraising glances? The divorce court records in the last ten years show that husbands sued by their wives on the euphemistic ground of "incompatibility" have been for the most part steady golf players or addicts to one or another form of muscular exertion. Why, to continue the embarrassing questioning, do professional athletes so often lose their wives to lounge-lizards, chauffeurs and barbers? Why, with a half dozen exceptions, have celebrated athletes been such failures, in after years, in business? Why, with the single exception of Jack London, who, at that, was pretty much of a muscular fraud, has no chronic exerciser written a good book or painted a decent picture or designed a sound building or composed even a respectable jazz tune in America in the last twenty-five years? The American, seeing pictures of John D. Rockefeller with a golf club in his hand and of George Bernard Shaw chopping at a block of wood, takes too much for granted. He fails to reflect that Rockefeller is the man he is because, once the kodak has snapped, it takes him three days, six masseurs and 480 to go around, and that Shaw is the man

he is, in turn, because the date on the picture showing him felling an oak is coincident with that of
Gabriele D'Annunzio's last bath.

§ 9

Muscle and Mentality.—College presidents are in
the habit of defending the late usurpation of the
scholastic curriculum by the gymnasium and
athletic field with the old Latin whangdoodle about
a healthy mind in a healthy body. The two actually
seldom go together. The fine minds are generally
to be found in bodies that are more or less constantly on their way to the drugstore or family
doctor. Fully two-thirds of the greatest geniuses
the world has produced have been physically defective. There isn't a life insurance company in
existence today that, assuming they were still in
mundane coat-tails, would take a chance on
Michelangelo, Beethoven, Shakespeare, Heine,
Mark Twain, Schumann, Molière, Robert Louis
Stevenson, Goethe, Stephen Crane, Cervantes, Swinburne, Strindberg, Ibsen, Chopin, Mozart, Händel,
Gluck, Samuel Johnson, Verlaine, Nietzsche, Laf-
cadio Hearn, De Quincey, de Musset, Wagner,

Paganini, Swift, Sardou, Ulysses S. Grant, Grover Cleveland or any one of a thousand other men whose names have gone into history's pages. All of these were of the sort that the Messrs. Strongfort and Muldoon presently address themselves to; not one of them could, in their lifetime, have made even a college freshman quoit-pitching team. College athletics may turn out successful realtors, bond salesmen, automobile agents and venders of radio sets, but if they turn out or ever have turned out minds one-hundredth so spectacular as their stock of biceps and calf-muscles I'd like a list of names and dates. The body is always developed at the expense of the mind, and all the eloquence of college presidents to the contrary convinces no one but the mentally deficient among the student body and the writers of sport news.

§ 10

Memorials.—One of the most foolish things in this foolish world is the erection of statues, shafts, monuments and memorials to members of the illustrious and venerated deceased. Not only is the practice foolish; more, it is insulting to the very persons it makes a show of honoring. The statue, the shaft or the monument itself may be all that the dead hero desires; it may be as much to his taste as if he had picked it out himself before being killed in battle, succumbing to heart failure while addressing the Chamber of Commerce of Bucyrus, Ohio, or being shot by the girl's fiancé. But though it may thus do honor to the dead hero in concept and intention, what does it do to him in actuality?

I answer the question by saying that nine times out of ten it flouts him, cheapens him, makes ribald mock of him, and disgraces his memory. Not intentionally, to be sure, but none the less absolutely. Look at any such monument that happens to be in your neighborhood and consider. Erected in admiration and humility out of funds subscribed to by all the local Elks, golf players, oil-stock salesmen and officials of the local branch of the National Security League, and dedicated with speeches by the leading local Jewish banker and Methodist clergyman and with Sousa marches by the Y. M. C. A. band, what happens long before even the two-dollar American flag and the five-dollar wreath of blooms that have been deposited upon it begin to fade? For the first few days, the natives come around to take a look at it, one or two of the more sentimental perhaps removing their derbies in its presence. The following Sunday, the local newspaper prints a large photograph of it, embellished with an inappropriate quotation from Milton. And then? Thenceforth the monument or statue or shaft or whatever it happens to be is completely forgotten and becomes for the rest of time by day a *châlet de nécessité* for dogs and by night an *al fresco* bordello for chauffeurs and servant girls. Or, if the memorial happens to be in a spot somewhat too conspicuous for amour, it generally soon becomes a stand for the sale of picture post-cards of the illustrious corpse and of paper-cutters, paper-weights, necktie clasps and suspender buckles bearing his image.

How a hero can find honor to him in such Rabelaisian and obscene uses to which his memorial is invariably put is something beyond my powers of appreciation. On that day when memorials to our heroes are put to other uses than garbage pails for banana skins, frankfurter ends and peanut shells, platforms for cheap political speeches and Fourth of July orations on the indivisibility of the Anglo-Saxon nations, public comfort stations for mutt dogs and baggageless hotels for concupiscent cops and cooks, on that day shall I perhaps at length persuade myself to permit my fellow countrymen, after my death, to honor me in the prevailing fashion.

§ 11

A Man Meditates.—What is at the bottom of a man's desire, albeit not always gratified, to retire from the morris dance of the world and spend his declining days in peace and quiet? That is, a man who has succeeded in his work in the world and has reaped amply the attendant rewards? The general idea—and in the general idea the man himself often concurs—is that he is growing old and no longer has zest for the game; that he deserves a rest; that, after all, his job has been done as well as he has known how to do it and that the applause the world has bestowed upon him is a sufficient glory to last him until the embalmer comes through the front gate. With due apologies, I privilege myself a loud hoot. What is back of such a man's impulse to withdraw from the world after he has tasted its tributes to his wisdom and sagacity is the knowledge that they don't amount to a damn and that only a relatively young man, still vain and foolish, can have any relish for them. The older man's ears have heard for years the indiscriminate handclappings and bravos of a pack of dolts, visited alike upon competence and incompetence, and he sees them for the trivial and absurd things they are. They are simply, he sees, toys with which strutting children in long trousers amuse themselves. And so his wish is to withdraw not from the true alarms of the world, with all their excitement, their challenge and their stimulation, but from the false alarms and the little celebrating popguns. The cottage by the still sea, the house on the lonely farm—these are not the refuges of age; they are the refuges from a world of adolescent celebrants, whose fireworks mean nothing.

§ 12

Seeing Things.—It occurs to me to speculate why the one kind of scientific man capable of writing a searching treatise on ghosts has never tackled the job. I allude to the ophthalmologist. Such a man, I believe, provided he devoted himself to a study of the subject and related his findings to his professional knowledge, might for once and all rid the world of much of the occult bosh that currently massages its belief in spirit manifestations. That many persons who say that they have seen ghosts are absolutely honest, that, indeed, they actually have seen ghosts, I have not the slightest doubt. For one fraud amongst them, I believe that there are a hundred who speak what is, to them, the truth. But that what they have seen are really ghosts, only an idiot, of course, could believe.

Ghosts or spirits, or what passes for them, are the results and conjurations of momentary defects in the human ocular system. They are illusions produced by momentary flaws and derangements in the human eye. With the complex machinery of this human eye, I am not overly familiar, and hence am not competent to say just what produces such temporary quirks and aberrations, just what throws the seeing apparatus out of true focus, and just what are the various nerve, stomach and other disorders that for the time being convert the eye

into a dubious instrument. But the experienced ophthalmologist is privy to such mysteries, and he
might handily correlate them with the ubiquitous
visions of deceased Uncle Henry, Little Bright Eyes
and other such members of the Order of the Celes-
tial Nightshirt.

When a woman wakes up suddenly in the middle
of the night and sees a ghost pointing a ghostly
finger at the ceiling, or mayhap only at papa's
union suit on the back of the chair, let the ophthalmologist jump into his Buick, rush post-haste to the
scene, and ascertain, by careful examination, just
what it is that has affected the functional delicacy
of her optic nerve. When a colored gentleman,
wandering about in a graveyard and already automatically sensitive to his surroundings, suddenly
lets out a yell at the vision of a slice of perambulating London fog, let an ophthalmologist in hiding
behind a tombstone hop out and take a look at the
manner in which his crystalline lens focuses upon
his retina. Let us have an examination of Sir
Arthur Conan Doyle's superior and inferior rectus
muscles, of Oliver Lodge's circular sinus or canal
of Schlemm, of the most recent Lombroso's *macula*

lutæ and *fovea centralis*. And we shall then have an end to a belief in spooks.

§ 13

Symbol Serfs.—Men are the masters of actuality and the slaves of symbols. For a cross, a flag, or a woman's name they will rush to lay down their lives, but they won't cough up a cent to lift the mortgage on the corner church, or stop guzzling enemy lager on the day of bloodiest battle, or keep their eyes from appraising the upstairs-maid's ankles.

§ 14

Ornithological Musing.—Perhaps the most persistent of legends is the theory that the noises of birds, commonly called singing, are musical. The notion has been born solely out of the sentimentality of love-smitten and befuddled numskulls. In such instances as a few first-rate musicians, *e. g.*, Beethoven, have employed bird sounds in their compositions, they have done so only in humorous, aye, in semi-derisory, terms. The best way in which to detect the utter absence of anything genuinely musical in a bird's chirpings is, curiously enough, since the method seems to have escaped persons almost entirely, to listen closely to them. If what issues from a bird's throat is melodious, then what issues from a nanny-goat's is a song by Schubert. The so-called singing of a bird, appraised by a man with a practised musical ear, is exactly and precisely of a piece with the sounds produced by an ungreased wheelbarrow axle. There is five times more genuine loveliness of tone in a river barge whistle, and ten times more in a soup spoon struck against a china bidet.

What deceives persons who hear music in the woodland chirpings and who look upon Bachman's sparrow, the junco, the Georgia swizzlegizzle and the Missouri wiffledingus as so many De Reszkés is a confusion of emotional reaction with the instrument that produces that reaction, a confounding of merely pleasant sounds with the tonal art. That the sounds made by a bird are soothing, ear-massaging, and even inspiriting, no more necessarily constitutes them music, in the strict sense of the word, than Delius' "On Hearing the First Cuckoo in Spring" constitutes a treatise on bird singing. It is only when musicians order the sounds of nature into melodious sequences, rhythms, harmonies and forms that they become music, as the sagacious *Musical Courier*, taking up the issue, points out. As examples there may be listed Alabieff's "The Nightingale," Jensen's "Murmuring Zephyr," Liszt's "Waldenrauschen" and Bendel's "Cascade of Chaudron," to say nothing of the gigantic Wagner's bird music in "Siegfried" and even his orchestral description of the growlings and bellowings of a dragon. The literal recording of nature's sounds, it need not be argued, is never music save it be filtered through the art of the musician. The persons who believe that the noises of birds are musical simply because they sound to them like music are the same persons who believe that the noises of Richard Strauss are not music because they don't sound musical to them.

"I find," says H. G. Wells in "The World of William Clissold," "the nightingales too abundant and very tiresome with their vain repetitions, but Clementina does not agree; her mind has been poisoned by literature, and she does not really hear the tedious noises they make, she hears Keats."

§ 15

The Waltz.—For the last fifteen years it has been steadily predicted, chiefly by persons who do not dance, that the waltz is due soon to return to favor and to supplant, in a measure, the current jazz antics. This prediction, I privilege myself to believe, is on a par with the other popular prediction that we will have light wines and beer back again within the next few years. The waltz will not return to favor for many years, and for a simple why and wherefore. Where in the yesterdays dancing was a diversion entered into with a more or less straight face, it has since become a pastime of low humor all compact. The minuet, the lancers, the schottische, the waltz, the polka and even the one-step were dances intrinsically devoid of gaiety and abandon and called for more or less dignity and reserve on the part of their participants. With the introduction of the two-step there dawned the first faint symptoms of the humor that has now reached its zenith in the jazz dance. The dance of today, accordingly, is entered into in a loose and jocular manner, like the baiting of colored gentlemen in the South and the eating of hot-dogs in the North. Grace, languor and formality have passed out of it completely. The dancing citizen has no use for them and gives no signs of having use for them. The waltz is utterly without humor and, being without this modern *sine qua non*, cannot possibly regain its hold until the entire attitude of a people toward its slippery-floor nonsense undergoes a radical change.

§ 16

Letters.—If ever I am called as a juror in a divorce case, or a suit for breach of promise, or a marriage annulment case, or a suit for separation, I shall cast my vote, whatever the general run of the evidence, against that one of the parties to the trial who has carefully preserved evidence over a long period of time in the form of letters written by the other. There is always something phoney about the person who saves potentially incriminating letters against a future day. His very anticipation of their usefulness is the mark of his premeditation and guilt. His act shows conclusively, it seems to me, his plan toward trouble. No honest man or woman in affairs of the heart preserves other of the other's letters save those that signify nothing but an affection that is and has been very beautiful. Letter-files are for business men and business women; the furnace is the only letter-file for honorable men and women when the subject before them is love.

§ 17

Classification.—The prevailing classification of human beings into rich and poor, successful and unsuccessful, strong and weak, master and slave, and so on, misses something. There is only one true, one exact, classification and that is the comfortable and the uncomfortable. Into one of these two pigeon-holes fall, with a sharp click, all men. The men who are comfortable in the world are the happy men; the men who are not are the unhappy and miserable. The rich man sometimes finds himself in the latter category, and so, too, do the successful man and the strong man. And, paradoxically, the relatively poor man who has not realized all his dreams, whose body is an ailing one and who is not entirely the master of his destinies sometimes finds himself in the former. The millionaire tormented by a dream he cannot realize, the successful man ridden by a shrew of a wife, the strong man outwitted by a weaker and more cunning one, these are men less comfortable than the poet singing his songs in a dog-hole, the hobo of the heart flirting easily with women along the road of life, or the Machiavelli with puny biceps. A Baron Rothschild, for all his fortune, is less comfortable than a pauper Franz Werfel, because, try desperately for years as he will, he still finds himself unable to write as Werfel can. A successful business man like Mellon, what with the irritations visited upon him by courts of law, is not as comfortable as the man who makes a peaceful living running some dinky little store around the corner. A Gene Tunney is perhaps for not more than two or three months a year as comfortable as the average man he could whip with one finger. All this, I duly appreciate, sounds like the dreadful stuff that the uplift magazines print, but nevertheless I believe that it has a considerable amount of truth in it.

§ 18

Beauty and Intelligence.—It has remained for Mr. Albert E. Wiggam, M.A., B.S., author of "The New Decalogue of Science," a gentleman who has attained to the mature age of fifty-five years, to contribute as his mite toward cosmic philosophy the doctrine that beauty and intelligence in women go hand in hand. Despite the fact that this revolutionary collop of news has been known to every reflective human being since small boys amused themselves sliding down the Esquiline Hill on their toga-seats, the legend that a beautiful woman is necessarily an ignoramus has enjoyed a curious persistence. The reason for the vitality of the legend is easily arrived at. In the battle of the sexes, the beautiful-intelligent woman enjoys odds of 100 to 1 over the man who would subjugate her to his bed, his board and his own anatomical loveliness. Thus, in order to make the scrap less one-sided, man has craftily spread the doctrine that beautiful women are utterly without sense, a doctrine that has been cultivated by him with such immense cleverness that the beautiful woman herself has actually been made to believe in it. As a result, there are very few women blessed with beauty who do not believe that their homelier sisters are privy to an intelligence that they themselves do not possess. Yet the homely woman, cruelly deprived of the fair's one's experience, generally knows much less than the pretty one. Her lack of good-looks, furthermore, makes a coward of her, and knowledge and courage are handmaidens. The homely woman gives the world its supply of schoolmarms and chambermaids. The beautiful woman gives the world its supply of Récamiers, Maintenons, Genlises, Staëls, Swetchines, Du Barrys and Nell Gwynns.

§ 19

Toujours Perdrix.—"Life would be endurable," observed Lord Palmerston, "if it were not for its pleasures." Like many another profound saying, this one has suffered because of its epigrammatic air and has accordingly been dismissed as being merely an amusing sample of smart-aleckry. Yet what reflective man of mature years does not appreciate its truth? The so-called pleasures of life, in the instance of each individual, are largely repetitive; they cuckoo one another more or less exactly from year to year, since a man's taste in such diversions changes little after he has crossed the line of thirty. In his younger years, these pleasures are still fresh and new to him; they have a kick that is infinitely agreeable; but, as time goes on, they lose their erstwhile appeal and gradually become transformed into bores. After thirty, the individual's pleasures fall into the grooves of his set predilections. Some of them are left-overs from his earlier years; others are of a relatively new contour. But, whatever their nature, he finds soon or late that they are in themselves very much of a piece and that each is but a recurrent echo of its former self. And presently each quondam pleasure becomes a stereotyped thing, to be undertaken, at best, in the half-light of duty. And, further, the indulgence in each of them becomes more and more irksome and peace-disturbing.

What are known by less experienced creatures

273

as pleasures, become, when the civilized man has reached forty, for the most part nuisances. Consider such hypothetical pleasures as dinner parties, banquets, receptions, teas, balls, weddings (of other persons), camping, athletic sports, flirtations, all-night drinking bouts, card games, musicales, excursions, three-day motor trips, picnics, college reunions, marching in parades, fighting policemen, and the like. What intelligent, or even half-way intelligent man, can extract amusement out of such things when he has reached his middle years? The answer is: no such man. But, none the less, such a man's life of necessity often includes the need of participating in one or more of these pseudo-pleasures, and he does so, obediently, politely and despairingly. And each participation makes him more and more miserable. Each invades his cherished privacy, his serious work in the world, his self-esteem. He is compelled to kiss brides whom he doesn't want to kiss, to drink more than he wants to drink, to go to places he doesn't want to go to, to speak soft nothings to women who he devoutly wishes were in Hell, to eat badly cooked dishes at dully peopled dinner tables, to hold leaking teacups on his lap and ruin his trousers, in short, to do countless things that seemed exceedingly agreeable once upon a time but that long since have become mildly obnoxious. Yet, such is the lamentable ridiculousness of human society, he must nevertheless keep on and on.

§ 20

The Civilized Man.—The phrase, "civilized man," appears to bother certain persons; a number of letters come in demanding an explanation. I venture a definition. The civilized man is one who believes that the pursuit of truth is the noblest of human occupations, but who freely confesses that, were he to catch up with it, he wouldn't know it if he saw it.

§ 21

The Censor Psyche.—Among the various motives that prompt a man to undertake the office of censoring the activities of his fellow men, one, I believe, has been overlooked by the Freuds. The first impulse of every human being, even before he is old enough to crawl out of his cradle, is to destroy.

The baby who bites vainly at his rubber teething-ring and beats his rattle violently against the cradle side is the precursor of the adult Methodist who snaps at elastic art and tries to break the silver sounds of the world's gaiety. The baby, growing into a boy, takes continued pleasure in breaking the window-panes of neighbors' houses, pulling out their doorbells, sticking a scissors into his sister's doll and disemboweling it of its sawdust, and smashing glass marbles to see just what produces the beautiful rainbow spirals within them. This boy is similarly the forerunner of the adult Methodist who derives his wayward pleasure from destruction of one sort or another. The boy, growing in turn into his late 'teens and even very early twenties, finds still a peculiar satisfaction in petty destructions and proves to be the best customer of clay-pipe shooting galleries, ball games in which he is vouchsafed three tries for a nickel at a negro's head, and other such diversions. This older boy, too, is but the Methodist on the way to maturity.

The men who devote themselves to censorship are simply men who have not, with the aid of experience, wisdom and honor, outgrown the childish desire for indiscriminate havoc. They are thus what may be designated emotional morons, human beings with adult bodies but with the minds, tastes and predilections of children. Unable to satisfy themselves with the species of destructiveness that pacified them in their earlier years, they cast about for new, legal and safe means to work off their moron steam and find what they are seeking in the arts. No longer able to derive any pleasure from breaking windows, they now attempt to achieve an emotional orgasm by breaking the creative work of a novelist or dramatist. No longer able to get any fun out of smashing a coon's skull with a baseball, they now try to calm their passion for demolition by putting spiked hurdles in the way of the artist.

§ 22

The Seed of Matrimony.—The theory that the man who commits matrimony, once his younger years have passed, does so because he finds his life increasingly lonely and hard to bear, enjoys a fructitude hardly warranted by the nonsense which waters it. Such a man generally marries not to escape loneliness but to achieve it. As a man gets

on in the world his daily life is invaded more
and more by outsiders of one sort and another;
his time is taken up more and more by persons
who harass and burden him with their kindly but
nuisanceful offices, with their genial and well-
meaning but tedious and irksome demands upon
his leisure, with their attempts to make him a
partner in gaieties and pleasures that he has no
taste for. He thus presently finds it almost impossible to get any time to himself, and he despairs.
What he craves is a barrier against these good-
natured but objectionable poachers, a shelter, if
only of relative degree, from these gregarious
friends, acquaintances and admirers. Marriage,
while certainly not the best barrier and shelter, is
better than any other that happens to be available,
and so he adopts it as a cure for his ills.

§ 23

Human Nature.—Not long ago, I wrote and published an article celebrating the many virtues of
a man I respect and admire, pausing only for a
moment in the eulogy to hint that, with all these
hundred-odd uncommon and enviable attributes

and qualities, he had also perhaps a couple of small faults. No sooner did the article appear than the object of my eulogy wrote and published a short article of his own, accusing me of simply growling at him.

§ 24

Free Speech.—The difficulty, thus far unsurmounted, to formulate a sound, satisfactory and workable definition of free speech is clearly to be appreciated after even a casual meditation of the problem. The truth, of course, is that the right of free speech is merely the dream of sentimentalists. Absolute free speech is an impossibility, and rightly so, in any even relatively civilized social organization or community. One might as well speak of free act, that is, the privilege of the individual not only to say anything he pleased but also to do anything he pleased. Take two champions of free speech, two men who advocate unchecked freedom of expressed opinion. One day, one of these champions confronts the other and tells him that his wife is a harlot. I need not indicate the prompt suppression of free speech on the part of the champion addressed. The illustration, to be sure, is a far-fetched and rather absurd one, but it betrays the first holes in the doctrine.

Civilization, of which social integrity, individual safety, the common amenities and the public welfare are, among other things, component parts, cannot abide free speech in the strict definition of the term. What staunch advocate of free speech amongst us would not hesitate over the privilege of a private approaching the general of the army at the height of conflict and telling him that he was all wrong in his tactical ideas and didn't know what he was doing? Prosperous and satisfactory conduct of government, on its highest and perhaps finest plane, is to be compared with the general in question, in other words, with competent autocracy. Free speech may go so far, and with undeniable profit, but it may not go farther. The man who, on a sinking liner, jumps into a life-boat, pushing aside a score of women and children and leaving them to drown, is simply a momentarily inarticulate free speaker; his suppressed words and opinions are as clear as if he shouted them at the top of his lungs. Take another and more relevant example. An advocate of free speech enters on a Sunday a church whose doors are open to the public and, in the midst of a prayer, stands up and proclaims that he does not believe in God. The man has and should have a perfect right to proclaim his belief, but the place where he does the proclaiming is not always his freely to select. He may do his proclaiming at home or in a barroom or on a public street-corner, but not in a place where he may properly and justifiably be arrested for disturbing the peace. Free speech is a mere empty phrase, therefore, save it be limited and conditioned by environment, scene and occasion. And when it is thus properly limited, it obviously and automatically becomes an even emptier phrase.

Although the framing of a comprehensively satisfactory definition of free speech has baffled talents infinitely greater than my humble own, I modestly offer just such a definition. Free speech, to wit, is and uninterruptedly should be on every conceivable occasion the prerogative of any and every citizen who is possessed of a sufficiently critical recognition of what has gone to constitute the soundest sociological, economic and individualist speculation that has antecedently come down to us. By this definition, plainly enough, the doctrine of free speech as a general privilege vanishes into thin air.

§ 25

Deceptio Visûs.—Various erudite editorial writers, carefully misreading certain animadversions of mine on the subject of censorship, have subtly contrived to make it appear that, because I have implied that among the hundred-odd nonsensical articles in the censors' canon there was conceivably one that had a modicum of sense and justification in it, I am therefore in favor of moral regulation of the arts. This logic is lamentably typical of controversial precedure as it obtains amongst us: the fence, however high and impregnable, is summed up in terms of its single knot-hole. To believe that a man is in favor of censorship simply because he says that there may be certain occasions when censorship may be intelligently defended by the censors themselves is to believe that a man is in favor of murder simply because he says that there may be certain occasions when capital punishment may be intelligently defended by its advocates.

The plain trouble lies not with censorship, but with censors. There isn't one of us, once his loud talk has died down, but believes in censorship in one degree or another. I should like to inquire of the stoutest foe of all censorship just what his attitude would be were a French peepshow, to which minors were freely admitted, to be opened on either side of his home. I should, further, like to make a similar inquiry of the staunchest opponent of theatrical censorship in the event that, let us say, the curtain to the dramatization of Dreiser's "An American Tragedy" were at one point kept aloft a few moments longer and the seduction episode in which Clyde and Roberta figure pursued with a Zolaesque realism. And I should like to continue the inquiry in the case of the loudest howler against literary censorship in the event that copies of John Cleland's immortal tome were published at a nickel each and sold freely to school-children. The way to beat censorship is not to deny all sense to it and all justification, but to give ground where ground must be given and then, when the enemy oversteps its bounds, to let fly at it with the full artillery of calm intelligence. The last way in the world in which to win a battle is to try to convince one's self that the enemy has no guns. To contend that the cause of art is in danger because the censors condemn and suppress a lot of dirty postcards, pornographic pamphlets, cheap moving pictures and equally cheap plays, to say nothing of a second-rate novel or so, is to make one's self and one's convictions ridiculous. Now and again, of course, a good piece of work suffers along with the contemptible ones because of the ignorance of the censors, but art is a poor and pitiable thing if it cannot survive such an occasional calamity. It has stood it in the past, and often enough. A relatively few years pass, the suppressed work duly comes into its own again, and all is as tranquil as it was before. True art simply can't be suppressed for long; history proves that much. If it can be suppressed and stay suppressed, you may rest assured that it isn't art. In all the centuries, not one genuinely fine piece of work has been suppressed by censorship for more than a little while. Art crushed to earth soon rises again.

Only the spurious in art remains lying in the dirt.

I am against censorship not because it is censorship, but because it is generally ignorant. I am against censors because, all the time, they disgrace the theory of censorship in its soundest sense and make it objectionable even to men who may be willing to grant its periodic integrity. I have before me two documents in illustration. One is a copy of an address, made recently on the floor of the House of Representatives by a Congressman from a Southern State, advocating a general censorship of magazines. After denouncing a certain magazine as immoral and corruptive, this would-be censor quoted at length, in chief and eloquent support of his case, an article which I myself had written, carefully omitting the name of the magazine in which it had appeared. Who among his hearers was to know that the article was published in the very magazine that he was denouncing? What is one to say of such open-and-shut hypocrisy and double-dealing? A second illustration is to be had in a letter lying on my desk as I write this. It comes to me from a gentleman of God and one of the two leading champions of censorship in

New York State. This holy gentleman, mistaking my attitude toward censors and censorship, observes that it is his opinion that the stage of New York City is unutterably filthy, that the law should be promptly and forcibly brought down upon it, and then asks me to supply him with the names of any plays that are dirty, confessing that he hasn't seen any of them himself! In other words, what we engage here is a censor who is certain that censorship is called for but who doesn't know what it is that should be censored. It is men like these—and they are typical of the tong—who bring censorship into vile disrepute and who cause all fair-minded and upright men and women to hold their noses. But let us get on our knees and thank God for them. It is they who are ruining irrevocably the cause of censorship amongst even censorship's more rational proponents.

§ 26

The Enemy Within the Gates.—Nothing is more dangerous to the security and welfare of a nation than an internal sense of humor. The moment a nation begins to show a talent for laughing criti-

cally at itself, however wise and profound the
mainspring of that laughter, that moment is it
doomed. To endure, a nation must be utterly
humorless so far as it itself is concerned. It may
mock and wax satirical at all the other nations of
the earth, but when it comes to itself it must be
as dully straight-faced as a division captain in the
heat of battle. The inability to laugh at itself has
preserved England for centuries, and made it
strong. The inability to snicker at itself is the greatest asset of America. Imagine how long the United
States would last were it gifted with a talent for
not taking seriously its current form of government, its hypocritical money-lender position in the
world, and its record—the real, honest-to-God, be-
tween-the-lines record—of its wars. Confidence is
born out of a nation's indomitable deficiency in
humorous self-criticism. But what then, says the
little bird, of pretentious Germany? Was it not
Germany's complete poverty in the direction of
esoteric mirth that led to its downfall? That is a
question that could only be asked by one who for-
gets that it was the late spokesman of the German
nation who observed, after a diatribe against what

passed for German depth, frankness and honesty: "Among ourselves alone we perhaps take the liberty to laugh at it all."

§ 27

Psalm 51.—Perhaps the saddest lot that can befall mortal man is to be the husband of a lady poet. It is, of course, bad enough to be a husband at all, so I am reliably informed by authorities, but to be the husband of a woman who squats on Pegasus and is pleasurably flicked by his tail must be the apex of human misery. The first year or so of such an alliance may not be unduly trying to the kind of man who can so much as look at a lady poet without a violent sinking of the tummy, but once life gets back into its usual humdrum the poor fellow's days must be filled with agony. It is not that he has to spend his nights, after he gets back from the day's grind at the shoe store or rolling-mills, listening to his wife's rhythmical inspirations about whippoorwills, nightingales and weeping-willows, but that he is compelled to listen for a very much greater period of time to her romantic tributes to lovers with which he often is hard put to it even vaguely to identify himself. He cannot for the life of him know whether her prosody is boosting him or some other fellow, either living or dead, real or imaginary. And if he is at all sensitive, it is not long before he takes to drink to salve his wounded pride.

The husband of a lady poet is soon or late doomed to be the butt of her Parnassian athletics. Long after other wives have quietly forgotten their husbands, he is forced to endure his spouse's slyly indirect criticisms of himself as a hot flame and, worse still, her eulogies of some other man as being all that he is not. It is the custom, I am told, of wives to refer lovingly and with a considerable nostalgia to their beaux of the days before they married, but surely no husband can find this half so katzenjammerish as a constant allusion, whether the verse be good or bad, to longed-for beaux of the future. The woman who marries a poet has an easier time of it, for the simple reason that a woman is capable of the technique of imagining herself to be even more beautiful and aphrodisiacal than any creature that her husband lyrically idealizes. But it is a rare man, once he has been married for a few years, who can persuade himself to find in his wife's idyls any analogy between himself and Benvenuto Cellini.

§ 28

Angosciosamente.—The American's hostility to what is beautiful and charming—a hostility as deeply rooted in him as his belief in the omnipotence of mazuma and God—finds its best illustration in a reconnaissance of all those originally placid and lovely spots of his own country which, with what would seem to be a flagellant's glee, he has debased and made hideous. There is today, with the exception of the Grand Canyon and Yellowstone Park, hardly one such beauty spot that he has left unsullied. He has taken the kingly magnificence of Niagara Falls, that mighty panorama of shooting silver and wind-waving green, and converted it into a mere sideshow for the legalized adulteries of yokels and the sale of picture postcards, tin medallions and souvenir garter buckles. He has taken Palm Beach, soft with the warm whisper of the tropics and lounging lazily by the tropical sea, and deafened it with jazz bands and the conversations of stockbrokers; and he has cut down its tall palms to put up bastard Andalusian villas and made its quiet sands a parade ground for ostentation and vulgarity. Atlantic City has been turned into what is nothing more than a three-mile-long hot-dog stand; Aiken and Hot Springs have been spread over with golf links for the delectation of opulent dolts; the Maine woods have been made indistinguishable from a New Jersey picnic ground, with sandwich remnants and the heels of dill pickles perfuming the pine-needled hills and with hundreds of canoes christened "Oh, Boy!", "Step-On-It" and "Hot Mama" infesting the lakes and streams; the Catskills have been turned into a synagogue and the Adirondacks into a lunger camp; New Orleans has been converted into a sort of Sam T. Jack's Creole show, with an annual shindig that is presently as Mardi Gras in spirit as an Asbury Park baby parade; and the entire State of California, excepting only two small slices, has been made over from a land of tranquil loveliness into one that is of a piece with the old Thompson and Dundy Luna Park, though without the latter's amusement possibilities. I pick out a few examples;

many others will readily occur to you. One and all they have been ruined by that spirit of æsthetic devastation that is the peculiar gift of our fellow-countrymen. One and all they have been devitalized of their natural charm and degraded.

The test of any place's charm, I daresay, is to imagine a civilized Continental being happy there. Try to imagine such a fellow at any of the places I have mentioned. Take California, for instance. The argument most commonly heard about California is that it would be all right if one's contemplation of the beauty of the scene were not regularly obstructed and offended by the presence of a retired Kansas or Iowa profiteer. This is largely a pose. A Kansas or Iowa ex-farmer may, true enough, be no lovely spectacle but, as human beings go in this world, he is surely no harder to look at than a Frenchman, and Frenchmen have never yet spoiled the French vista. What has ruined California, save in two spots, is not the presence of these American images of Jehovah but the mood that they have brought into the State with them. The mood of California, even up to ten years ago, was one of easy and gracious peace. Today, it is that of an Elk driving a Ford. Where once were orange groves are now only realty development projects. Along the once undefiled southern coast, a Riviera transplanted to the Pacific, are now thousands of red-painted atrocities heralding the merits of women's brassières and men's smoking tobaccos. Everywhere are ten-cent rollercoasters, hit-the-nigger-in-the-head games, shoot-the-chutes and Ferris wheels. The highways are dotted with Wichita-Mexican and Omaha-Spanish architectural debauches. Down the lovely winding sea road toward Playa del Reyo and San Pedro, on a high green wooded hill overlooking the arm of the ocean that reaches out to enfold within it the most beautiful coast line this side of Port Limon and Costa Rica, there stands—a tearoom!

§ 29

The Need For Illusion.—The greater the realist, the greater his need for illusion in order to stand life at all. This illusion a Zola finds hidden in the wines of the Château Beauséjour, a Hauptmann in periodic quilldriving excursions into fairy tales, a Nietzsche in the verse of sentimental German rhymesters. A world rid of its ritualistic churches, theatres, wine-cellars, pretty telephone girls and poets would blow up, out of its own despair, by nightfall.

A NOTE ON THE TYPE IN
WHICH THIS BOOK IS SET

This book is composed on the Linotype in Bodoni, so-called after its designer, Giambattista Bodoni (1740–1813) a celebrated Italian scholar and printer. Bodoni planned his type especially for use on the more smoothly finished papers that came into vogue late in the eighteenth century and drew his letters with a mechanical regularity that is readily apparent on comparison with the less formal old style. Other characteristics that will be noted are the square serifs without fillet and the marked contrast between the light and heavy strokes.

SET UP, ELECTROTYPED AND PRINTED
BY THE VAIL-BALLOU PRESS, INC.,
BINGHAMTON, N. Y. · ESPARTO
PAPER MANUFACTURED IN SCOT-
LAND, AND FURNISHED BY W.
F. ETHERINGTON & CO.,
NEW YORK · BOUND BY
H. WOLFF ESTATE,
NEW YORK.